How God Does Diversity

A thought for every day of the Year

Tim Daniel

© 2025 Timothy Daniel
All rights reserved.
NO AI TRAINING
ISBN 9798218849252
Library of Congress Control Number: 2025924528
Cover photo by Dulcey Lima on Unsplash
First Edition 2025

Acknowledgements

To my wise host, who somehow knew I was ready to enter a new world.

Prologue

I was an exchange student in a foreign country. It was an immersion experience. I lived with a family that spoke a different language than my own as their first language. My language school taught the new language in the new language without any translation into or from my first language. The other students were from seven different countries so there wasn't one language we shared besides the new one we were learning. The new language was our pathway into full participation in the society where we now lived. I arrived in late Day and began classes around the first of Day. My host and hostess spoke my language as a second language and were able to translate for me when I was confused.

One morning in mid-Day, my host kindly but firmly informed me they would no longer translate for me - starting that day. It was time. If I did not use what I had already learned it would never congeal in my head.

By doing the best I could with what I already had I rapidly gained working fluency. If my host and hostess had continued translating for me I would have remained stuck between two worlds, unable to return to my old one and unable to enter my new one with any degree of freedom and confidence. With one gentle but firm shove, he effectively led me out of a state of safe but unnecessary prolonged dependence into a state of scary but exciting independence.

To my astonishment, one wonderful day a few months later I realized I was thinking in the new language without translating. What was once a jumble of noise around me as people talked on the train was now full of meaning. I felt connected to a community of lives just by overhearing their normal chatter about normal things.

It was all so much easier and fun. Now I could think thoughts and feel feelings my own language did not permit. I even began to dream in the new language.

If you have learned something about how God does happiness you have a new goal for living. If you have learned how God does change you have a new way of reaching and entering that new way of living. Now is the time to put all that to use. No more translating. We will do very little if any contrasting this way of living with the any other way of living. For those of us who are different there is no other way of living.

We will speak from this point forward in our own language about our own concerns. From here we go both deeper and higher into our own new world.

Day 1

In nature, God's creatures do the right thing for themselves, their own kind, and their habitat. Evolution, another of God's masterpieces, made them that way.

With one exception: when they become infected with disease. Mammals infected by rabies no longer act "correctly" - they attack other animals for no reason; they lose their healthy and protective sense of fear and become rabid.

When plants get infected with insect or soil borne diseases they stop functioning properly. Their leaves brown or turn brittle, their fruits rot and eventually they die because so much of their leaf surface is damaged that they can't photosynthesize anymore.

Disease is as much a part of the story of life as health. So is life's response to disease. We are part of life's response to disease. Evolution made us that way. We can't *not* do something about it and be happy.

Day 2

The entire human species is susceptible to a fatal social disease. Once caught, it can do lasting epigenetic damage. Once the disease spreads through a population, rather than the exception being a poorly or oddly functioning individual, it becomes the norm to act like a rabid groundhog, Once infected, we behave contrary to how we were designed to function and destroy a natural way of living that is healthy, helpful and cooperative.

The infection causes unwarranted certainty about what is best and then unlimited wanting, allowing no barrier to what we are just sure will make us happy. The disease takes on a life of its own and builds itself up into an entire civilization that is as destructive as it is unnatural.

Yet somehow, a few rare humans still have something in their DNA that fights back against the disease.

Day 3

Those with the functioning remains of moral immune response first become selfish, unhelpful, and uncooperative any time they want something, just like everyone else. But they feel sick inside when they behave this way. Eventually they can't go on this way and cry out to their Maker for help. They seek God directly, not a representation of God.

Upon making direct and constant contact with God, slowly they become less willful and selfish. They stop seeking to get as much as possible from others while giving little or nothing in return. They start to find ways to be helpful and cooperative. They seek to increase the stock of happiness around them, so everyone has more to draw on. They do this at their own cost in terms of time, attention, and care even though they often receive no help in return.

They have learned that God replenishes them daily and then some, and usually in unexpected ways. It is more than enough. This allows them to keep becoming increasingly cooperative and helpful.

Day 4

Social species survive planet-wide population reducing events through cooperation, not through selfish savage competition.

If you are recovering from the disease and are becoming naturally cooperative you feel better, you sleep better, but now you are out of step with those around you.

You are different.

You are part of a very small, rapidly diminishing minority. You have been excluded and pushed to the margins by the majority. This is both natural and necessary.

Day 5

When a deadly infection has damaged an entire species God quarantines the few who have demonstrated the ability to throw off the disease. The lucky few carry the cure in their instinctive values and behaviors, so God removes them and preserves them in safety.

Meanwhile, devastation awaits a rabid species of selfish, uncooperative competitors, each taking everything possible and giving nothing back beyond empty promises and cheap gestures.

When a big crisis arrives, they will find themselves unwilling and unable to work together to overcome it. Each individual and each group will demand that others help and cooperate but will reserve the right to refuse to help and cooperate themselves.

Day 6

While in quarantine we must not lose our most vital capacity; the ability to create and maintain a shared well-being with other creatures.

Capacities we don't' use wither away. The capacities we use so constantly they have no time to replenish themselves drain away.

In quarantine, God keeps us in a middle state in between idleness and burnout. We neither waste away nor waste our lives on efforts that have no chance of making any lasting difference.

Day 7

To remain fully functional, we must be in a situation that applies constant pressure but not crushing pressure.

God designed our brains to avoid wasting energy, since the brain is a very energy-hungry organ. As a result, we respond with real adaptive learning only when a threat or opportunity is measurably real, not when it is imaginary.

Day 8

To remain healthy, we must feel the pressure that comes from the possibility of real loss should we make an unwise choice.

Feeling vulnerable does not mean we have done something wrong; rather it means God is keeping us alert, receptive and responsive.

To remain healthy, we choose to live in a state of managed vulnerability, making daily choices under God's direction to stay within God's ethical limits.

Day 9

There will always be an enticing method to throw off the pressure entirely and become invulnerable. The problem is the method will require harming another creature that has done nothing to harm us.

To never feel vulnerable again, we must hoard more resources than we will need any time soon. The only way to do this is to take from other lives what they need right now or will need soon, while giving nothing of real value in return.

This leaves other lives without reserves to draw upon when times of great stress arrive, which will happen.

Day 10

Even though it is foolish in the long run for any creature to achieve invulnerability by making other creatures more vulnerable, it is still enticing and very possible to do – for a while. We must learn to recognize the first signs of the disease.

We have become infected with uncooperative selfishness if:

- We no longer feel the need to seek or depend on God for guidance.
- We feel we have all the answers now.
- We no longer have any desire to learn from nature.
- We only want to learn from other humans.
- We are unwilling to wrestle with our conscience and with each other to find an ethical solution to our problems, because doing so might cost us comfort and ease.

If these attitudes come to prevail over us, functionally, for the time being we are no longer different. We are now carriers of the disease, even if we work in professions that profess to improve humanity.

Yet God made a few of us so deeply different that we eventually throw off the disease.

As we recover we see that...

God does happiness differently.
God does change differently.

After recovering we can serve as part of the earth's immune system and be carriers of the cure.

In nature, what can overcome existential danger originates exactly where and when there once was existential danger. Cures do not arise in a place and time of comfortable safety.

Day 11

The minute we start to feel smug and snug in our clever invulnerability our constructive creative capacities start to wither away, creating a painful vacuum.

Destructive creative capabilities begin to grow in the vacuum we have created.

The temptation to be invulnerable, to never struggle again, is the entry point of the disease that leads to extinction. To achieve invulnerability, we must refuse to care about or cooperate with other of God's creatures, human and otherwise.

Day 12

What makes us different is the growing will and skill to resist the temptation to become invulnerable at the expense of other creatures.

This difference is why God selected and quarantined us. If we lose this difference we lose God's involvement with us. There is no greater loss, as it leads inevitably to the loss of everything else.

God will not permit us to lose what we have been given. God will stop and correct us when we start down the road of selfishness. God's discipline is proof we have been selected and preserved for a purpose beyond our own personal comfort.

God's firm rebuke and gentle redirection is the surest sign one has a divine calling.

Day 13

God's discipline usually comes in the form of a painful experience that is the natural consequence of selfish, uncooperative behavior. It is so painful that we never want to do anything like that again.

We learn to accept God's discipline and embrace the struggle to survive while staying within ethical limits.

God's discipline keeps us different in a way that makes a difference in the lives around us. Others find we are not interchangeable with the average person out there who is equally qualified on paper. We bring a dynamic to the mix others don't. When we leave others notice a drop in their quality of life and work.

Day 14

We learn not to take from other lives, either by force or cunning, what God provided for their survival and growth. We don't bully and we don't mislead others to meet our needs. Instead, we call out to God and God answers. We accept and engage in the struggle to find another way.

This repeated situational/ethical/creative problem-solving experience is itself a divine that trains us and then keeps us uniquely useful to God so we can be helpful to life.

Our training instills in us reflexive behaviors that leave us out of step with the majority, but that allow us to retain and grow our place on earth, during our time on earth.

Day 15

To participate fruitfully in how God does diversity it helps to understand why God does diversity – to create options. In a changing situation it is always better to have more and better options than fewer and worse options.

God designed life with the ability to create and preserve a wide range of options for survival as conditions on earth change. Diversity is that collection of options life itself created and appears in the form of differentness, in ways of behaving that are new and misunderstood at first, but don't need to harm any other life.

Day 16

Variety is the secret that keeps life open-ended and evolving. Life always keeps in reserve a few functioning prototypes who are uniquely suited to somehow sustain themselves through the current devastation and then begin again.

The preserved prototypes go on to build something very different from what existed before the catastrophe.

Day 17

Identity is key to diversity. We discover who we really are by first discovering who we are not. We must discover where we belong by first experiencing where we don't belong.

Taking on a packaged identity already available is a kind of shopping. We adopt what someone else created. We learn it is different from making the most of what God gave us and no one else, because it is not satisfying for very long.

In God's economy, each individual's deepest satisfaction is unique and unreplaceable.

Adopting the identity of a group is like trying on clothes to see if they fit. We learn who God designed us to be by first learning who God did not design us to be, so it is common to pass through various groups with established norms people expect us to emulate.

Day 18

With each group we pass through we gain a deeper understanding of the mystery of our own uniqueness. We pick up some things that help us express God's design, and we discard some things that don't.

Within each group we find some degree of selfishness and uncooperative behavior. We find there is no group we can run to where the sickness has not already arrived.

Day 19

We discover that having found a group in which everyone appears to be like us on the surface is different from following God's guidance to discover who we really are.

A moment comes when something inside us pulls in one direction ethically, and our group pulls us in the opposite direction.

We feel torn. We must choose between God's approval and support and our group's approval and support. We start to suspect this may not be where we belong forever.

Day 20

Each time we choose God's ethical priorities over our group's acceptance and support we lose some standing in the group, but we gain more of our authentic, original identity and purpose.

It is hard to imagine it is a good trade off, but in time we come to see it is. God somehow sustains us, but our material preferences must change so we don't become resentful and envious.

Day 21

We discover that a spartan, safe cabin with a basic meal plan on a freighter headed to the right harbor is better than a luxury cabin with fabulous buffets and entertainment on a cruise ship headed to the wrong harbor.

God knows a storm is coming that will sink every ship in the wrong harbor. God uses unforeseen events to guide us to a safe harbor.

God acts in mercy to preserve us in safety, not in luxury.

Day 22

Our sense of affinity and belonging shifts along with our sense of identity. Somehow we find other recovering cooperators along the way. We meet in ways that are always unforeseen, unplanned, unprogrammed.

We start to see that unpredictability is the pathway of God's ongoing creation.

We bond with each other in the same unpredictable, unscripted way.

Day 23

Each new, mutually beneficial, helpful relationship takes form under circumstances that cannot be replicated. Our bonds are no less real because they can't be bottled and distributed, in fact they are the only ones that are real. It is the way of nature.

There are no assembly lines in nature. Yet there is one constant, survival through struggle, change and cooperation.

Day 24

With a new identity comes a new, surprising experience of belonging.

The more we become uniquely who God designed each of us to be individually by participating in the new cooperative relationships God entrusts to us, we find to we are more like our new companions from different groups, than the unhelpful, uncooperative members of the group we grew up in.

Day 25

In nature diverse forms of life arise from unique local habitats called niches. No niches, no diversity, no diversity, no survival when something big and deadly arrives.

A niche is a place where you can sustain yourself and those you love without harming anyone. In fact, your small niche is a place where your instinctive helpfulness, your desire to create and protect cooperative relationships is precisely what those around you value and reward.

Day 26

Niches are hiding places, hidden from the hurried eye but visible to the patient eye. The hurried eye sees what is in the situation now. The patient eye sees the pattern in what is in the situation over time, knowing that nothing stays the way it is right now forever.

The whole point is to be invisible to those who would do us harm. Relative safety, sufficient stability, and the need for constant development of new skills – these are the benefits provided by a niche. We don't expect or seek more than that. Instead, we make the most of those benefits.

In your niche and only in your niche, you will become an ever more fully developed version of what you are. You will unfold into a design you have seen in no other life, because God did not place you where you are so you could copy another life.

Day 27

As you respond to God's training to meet the needs you find in your niche, your growth will take on a trajectory. You get hints at where your life may be leading. It is enough to keep you moving and engaged.

God uses signals and hints to direct our interest, attention, and effort toward an unfolding mystery. In the process our lives become a unique work of elegant, functional, and beautiful design – the very fingerprint of God.

The mystery of our identity unfolds in response to specific situations, managing our way through events that we cannot foresee or cause. Imagined stories about things that never happened to people who never lived start to lose their attraction.

The most interesting story we can find starts to be our own.

Day 28

With eager anticipation we turn the page each morning to see what happens next. We find it about half blank. One half has our duties written on it. The other half has open space under the heading of unresolved problems and unanswered questions.

Through each act of listening obedience to God we slowly fill in the open spaces with solutions that are new, unforeseen, and better than any options we already know about.

As God grows us into our own unique design we find we become more functional than not, more functional than we used to be, and more functional than most people. The chaos in and around us starts to quiet into a surprising, different, and higher order than we imagined and pursued before.

Day 29

You are deeply different anyway so there is no reason not to become fully differentiated. If you are in the niche God set aside for you, you become more valuable to others the more you become all God designed you alone to be. It is hard to believe, but it is true!

You will be more accepted as you learn to do masterfully all God gave you the innate desire and talent to do. Your fully developed uniqueness will secure your place and earn your status among other recovered and preserved cooperators.

Day 30

There is genius in where God places us. If a niche is too far from where the infection of selfish non-cooperation rages, we will not develop the ability to recognize and overcome the infection when it comes into our environment.

If we try to build a life too near the center of the infection nothing we do will be enough to avoid getting sick ourselves.

A society of selfish competitors will change us before we change them and more than we change them.

Day 31

God does not expect us to be naïve and innocent, never having seen or been touched by cunning selfishness. That would leave us defenseless and angry at God when we inevitably interact with those who seem to be winning the game of life through cheating.

Instead, God calls us to be realistic and relevant, able to survive direct contact with cunning selfishness with our helpful instincts intact. After contact with the disease, that which makes us different is even stronger and more ready to respond the next time.

To fit us to our calling, God places us in a niche that lies in the middle zone, between too much contact with the disease of uncooperative selfishness, and too little contact with it.

Day 32

It is important to have enough distance from the quarreling competitors to see the larger pattern that unfolds when a human group is made up of nothing but individuals out for themselves alone.

Living in the middle zone we get to see first-hand how the contest between selfishness and helpfulness plays out over time, not just who seems to be winning at the moment.

God does not ask us to completely seclude ourselves behind walls. When dealing with a threat that is everywhere and can gain access anywhere at any time, walls don't protect. Wisdom is the only thing that can protect us, God's wisdom.

We live near the infected, we know the players personally and have had repeated dealings with them. We can quickly spot the early signs of infection.

Day 33

Because God places us in the middle zone, we don't have to rely primarily on the opinions of remote experts, on hearsay, or published reports to see the pattern of selfish living. We don't need to use those sources to make our case for God's very different way of living.

By relying on our own direct experience, we gain a natural authority and confidence we can't gain from trusting second-hand sources.

Day 34

The ability to do first-hand, long-term observation is a natural capacity that is essential to regrow and practice if we want to fully recover and stay healthy as a society. As we recover from the disease of uncooperative selfishness we no longer observe using only the *impatient eye*.

The impatient eye sees what we can grab and hoard right now and overlooks who gets hurt.

Day 35

We learn to see with the *patient eye* that gathers information over time. We see the chain of consequences that follow choices. We start to see the pattern starting to form early.

If we can predict from experience that the consequences of a choice are harmful to life over time. We seek God to make a better choice.

God guides us to do something different than everyone else does, who are simply imitating each other.

We will use the recovered *patient eye* capacity to solve almost every problem we will encounter as we found a new civilization, so God makes sure we encounter lots of situations that require us to use and develop that capacity.

Day 36

Quarantine is not designed to be comfortable or pleasurable. During an epidemic we must adjust our preferences. We would prefer to have company, but infected company is dangerous.

During an epidemic solitude is preferrable to sick company. But once God brings others into our lives who are also recovering from the disease, their company is preferrable to solitude.

Day 37

Those of us who are recovering cooperators can form new clusters of cooperation. Our clusters can help each other, as each one is learning to do something important that the others can learn to do better and vice versa.

God expands life through diversity. In destructive times, God preserves the next, stronger forms of life through quarantine. Being somewhat marginalized and excluded protects us. Gaining standing and equity in a group of selfish competitors is like winning a nicer cabin on a sinking ship.

It is a change in our situation that doesn't make a decisive difference in the long run. Rather, it is a lethal strategy.

Day 38

Humans are different from each other in thousands of ways, large and small. If we are not cooperative, those differences drive us apart and pit us against each other. If we are cooperative, God brings our vast differences together in a tensed productive unity in which all of us have what we need to survive and thrive.

To be cooperative is to be different in a way that is critical for life on earth to continue and unfold as God intended. All other differences combined, as wonderful as they are, lose their impact without a change in how we cooperate with one another.

Day 39

Once God has changed us and taught us how happiness really works, we are helpful and cooperative, not as a temporary tactic to get something. Rather, we are cooperative as a constant way of responding to whatever happens in us, to us, between us and around us.

Something so constant and persistent can't be produced solely by teaching, learning, and modeling. Nor can it be motivated and sustained solely by incentives. Only a natural, ancient adaptive trait has the power to pass on and sustain a distinctive behavior with or without social support.

Day 40

God is merciful. God has not abandoned any part of humanity, regardless of their cultural differences without natural path back to what God intended for all humans.

A lucky few in every human group across the globe still possess the cooperative trait. It has been repressed by an environment that only rewards selfishness. It has lain dormant, but it awakens under the stress of adversity and resets our priorities from the inside out.

We may not feel very lucky while the reset is happening, but with the patient eye we come to be happy that we are so deeply different.

The root word of happy is "hap." "Hap" means lucky.

Day 41

Those of us with this dormant cooperative trait got the selfish sickness too but somehow God activated something powerful buried deep inside us; fond memories from childhood that the Creator is real, powerful, and benevolent.

We remember the God we once loved, and we call out to the God we remember. Somehow God rescues us. First from the inside out, then from the outside in. God changes our situation to one that is initially harder, but one in which requires ethical faithfulness. We find choosing what is right is both possible and pivotal.

We have experienced first-hand how God does change so we can experience how God does happiness. In the process we have become resiliently helpful, hopeful, and cooperative.

Day 42

Since God is in charge, knows everything, is everywhere in everything, can do anything, and if we remain firmly on God's side in the struggle for the future of earth – we can be hopeful without being delusional. We know we are on the side that will ultimately win.

Without realistic hope it is rational to feel helpless. Without realistic hope it is rational to be unhelpful. Why put out the effort to help someone else when everything is going to fall apart anyway?

With realistic hope it is rational to take responsibility for ourselves and be helpful to others.

Day 43

Being deeply cooperative is a God-given trait. It is as much a part of nature as the white blood cells distributed across our bodies and serves much the same purpose.

Since God made us this way, God alone can teach us how to manage being like this. We are part of a vast design we can't even begin to grasp, but one we can sense exists and can participate in it fully.

Being different has cost us dearly. Yet somehow our reserves are constantly replenished. We could have become permanently bitter. It is very human to become bitter and cynical when our trust is betrayed, and our help goes unreturned.

Somehow that didn't happen or if it did, it didn't last.

Day 44

We are human. We too became bitter for a time. But something in us would not let us stay that way. We sought God. God met us and taught us. God helped us in ways we never could have predicted, planned, controlled, replicated, or packaged for sale.

Clearly, what is going on is far bigger than any of our personal stories or the story of any one group or species. Our differentness is like a piece of steel inside us that pulled toward a powerful magnet outside us. We feel ourselves drawn into a vast, ancient, and unstoppable story. Like a tangled rope pulled across a table, the closer we are drawn to God the more our lives straighten out to serve their function.

As we learn more about what God is up to, we sense we being pulled toward our true home.

Day 45

As we are pulled ever deeper into God's design for earth, we sense that we belong. Here, finally, we have standing and a purpose. Our lives matter uniquely. Our days are often very interesting.

We have these treasures precisely because of what makes us different from the still-infected majority.

Collectively, scattered across the globe in small working units, we form the seed bank for a radically new civilization, one designed from the very beginning to help life and further the hidden purposes of God.

Day 46

God's astonishing design becomes clearer only as it unfolds - through one choice, one solution at a time. The solutions are often re-solutions of old unresolved issues.

Scientists have often solved an old problem by using a new, higher-resolution device to extend their senses. With the older, lower-resolution device distinctions were blurred, so that two things looked like one thing.

Once we see two distinct phenomena separately we realize there is not one solution that will address both. Each requires its own fitted solution. From there a path to something better opens.

Day 47

We seek and receive daily ethical guidance from God only in our struggles to respond to complex, changing, and difficult situations. We are patient. We observe carefully until we see distinctions and causes. We experiment until we figure out what works and yields the peace of God.

Each of these hard-won, original, learned responses prepare us to effectively meet coming conditions and events, currently known only to God.

As a result, over time, where others see only the certainty of meaningless suffering, we see the raw material and rough outline for a new, better way of living together in justice. We know God's peace inside and bring divine peace into the messy situations we encounter.

Day 48

God does not ask us to stop being different so we can fit in with the still sickened majority any more than a doctor would ask a healthy patient to catch a virus to better fit in with the dying patients in the ICU.

God also does not ask us to stay different and try to win the attention and approval of the sickened majority.

The sickness of uncooperative selfishness prevents the infected from seeing anything more than sentimental value in our recovering ability to cooperate and help each other.

Day 49

What God does ask us to do is make the most of what makes us different.

Our job is to grow our natural desire and ability to cooperate to its full strength. We are drawn to follow our instinct to build cooperative relationships in places where it is still possible and necessary to create cooperative relationships.

The pull of God's rule in our hearts moves us out of places where it is no longer possible to build helpful, cooperative relationships. We move from provided niche to provided niche over a lifetime, each one bringing out more of what God put in us.

Day 50

Once recovered, our job in quarantine is to become very skilled at what comes naturally to us, knowing how to use what God gave us to meet every new challenge we encounter.

As we grow into full maturity we become to human systems what beavers are to natural systems. As we do what comes naturally to us, a whole new thriving social habitat takes shape, one that supports more life, more types of life, and more communities of life.

With us in the mix, diversity gently thrives in the warmth of God's delight.

Day 51

Before the Wright Brothers figured it out, there were many other types of experimental aircraft that failed. They could not fly twice. It did not matter what color they were painted.

Color was a difference that made no difference in the achievement of mechanical flight. These fatally flawed aircraft crashed on their first flight because they lacked the few essential design features that make flight possible and safe.

Day 52

In the Wright Brothers' airplane, each essential design feature imitated something a bird's body can do to respond to the real but invisible forces that act on a body up in the air.

In a similar way, under God's changing touch, we come to live out a cluster of behaviors that together form the critical difference between a species going extinct and one that lives on as part of earth.

By seeking and responding to God's ethical touch daily, we acquire the ability to overcome the gravity of uncooperative selfishness. We learn to stay in an elevated ethical state while moving forward into whatever the future holds. We bring God's rule into future with us through every choice we make today that affects the lives of others.

Day 53

In God's design for humanity there is one feature that pulls all the others together into a functioning ethical cluster. What allows all our amazing capacities to fulfill their function is the method of knowledge acquisition other creatures use in nature. Infected humans think they are smarter than other creatures. Recovering humans can sense it is the other way around.

Without God's natural way of acquiring knowledge, we inevitably misuse our capacities and do harm.

Day 54

There is a natural, healthy way of knowing what is true and what Is not true in any situation. As long as we know enough about what is true and what is not true, we can successfully undertake any challenge God assigns to us.

We spare no effort in mastering God's natural method to know what is true, so we can know what to do. We must first learn what not to do and why. Unlearning what not to do is hard because it requires a lot of time and effort, and we seem to have nothing to show for it.

But that is not true. What we have left after unlearning what not to do is an empty, blank canvass. Unlearning produces openness. It clears a once obstructed channel we then use to communicate with God and listen to others.

Day 55

All creation starts with nothingness. Only God can bring something out of nothing. Once we are open, clinging to nothing but God, we are in for the lesson of our lives.

What materials do we need to learn God's method of knowledge acquisition? Our own unique, intimate situation. That includes the chaos that goes on both inside and outside our heads.

Only God can bring beautiful, functional order out of chaos. By God's side and on God's side in the struggle, we witness the emergence of something new, different, and better than what was there before.

Day 56

The niche God placed us in contains in its every frustrating detail all that we need to discover how God does and does not bring reliable information into our lives. If God gives a situation to us, God guides us in that situation and shows how to work out a graceful new way to deal with it. And it is a lot of work.

It seems that second-hand representations from experts who are not here with us right could save us some of the work of figuring out what is true and what is right to do. We are human. Humans like to save effort any time they can.

But we lose more than we gain if we let others do our thinking for us. We lose the ability and willingness to think through complex problems, making us useless to God in service of life.

Day 57

It is tempting to trust someone else's work rather than do our own work to understand what causes good and bad things to happen, and what we must adjust to prevent the bad and set the good in motion in our situation.

We soon find ourselves confused by second-hand representations of what causes bad and good things to happen, created by people we don't know. What we have been told doesn't agree with what we are observing. We must spend time and energy deciding which to trust, the word of remote experts or our own eyes, ears, and logic.

This confusion makes it harder to make good choices and delays the process of figuring things out. This is not God's knowledge acquisition method.

Instead, what is measurably or observably here now contains the most important clues we will use to make the best choice possible in time to make a difference.

Day 58

We learn this rule by heart: What is given by God will be guided and graced by God. What is not given by God will not be guided or graced by God.

When God does not go before us, creating openings, we find must use force or deception to move our solutions forward. We must harden our hearts to the harm we cause to the innocent. Doing so feels dis-graceful. Since we don't want to feel disgraced again, since we don't want to become callous and indifferent, we don't repeat those tactics.

When and where God guides and graces, God creates openings. We wait and watch until the opening appears, then move through with no need to bully or mislead.

We learn to spot the difference quickly between methods God will assist and those God will not assist.

Day 59

Grace is what we see in the motions of a butterfly or gazelle. Grace is the precise use of energy for a specific purpose at a specific time in a specific place. Gracefulness is fitting action to need, exactly when, where, and how it is needed, for exactly how long it is needed and no longer. Grace and rigidity are mutually exclusive.

A graced action is most often fresh and original. Afterwards we realize it was so perfect it feels like it was inevitable, as it opened a new chapter in our situation.

Day 60

Graceful, guided, precisely timed, decisive action is the way humans participate in the ongoing work of creation.

We learn that if we chase and grab something, motivated by greed, fear or envy, the effort will not be guided, nor will it be graced.

At the very least our efforts will be an exercise in futility, but often our efforts turn out to be destructive to ourselves and others.

Day 61

There is a way of doing diversity that is not God's way, which we learn to avoid.

We learn that when we attempt to be different in the same way an existing group of people is different – by definition, we are not different. Rather, we become just one more of them, essentially interchangeable with any member of that group. We quickly realize that once you've seen or heard one of them, you've seen and heard all of them.

There is something about mimicking an existing group's behaviors that is somehow less interesting and satisfying than being part of the rich, surprising, ever-evolving diversity we see in nature.

By following God's ethical guidance daily, we find that discovering our own unique identity is far better than mimicking!

Day 62

Using the patient eye and falling silent so we can listen deeply - we absorb the fact that nowhere in nature does God pump out copies of a standard type. Instead, God creates originals.

To participate in God's remarkable process of original creation, we keep moving until we find unique, evolving individuals who are also moving in the same direction we are, in the same ethical way, for the same honorable reason.

We meet others who also want to be live closer to God and behave in cooperative ways like what they see in natural systems. They bring things to the effort we don't and vice versa.

Day 63

We know we have met someone who is also recovering from the disease of uncooperative selfishness, when we see clear signs of recovered health in our first encounter:

Courtesy.

Listening.

Modesty.

Patience.

Day 64

God made us a social species. We naturally long for stable relationships with people we can trust, rely upon, and admire. Earth is one of God's masterpieces in the universe, extremely rare and possibly unique in its ability to support complex life. A restored earthling is another of God's masterpieces – rare, elegant, and effective.

Forming a bond with such a person is easy, enjoyable, and natural.

When dealing with another whom God is restoring to moral health, it is striking what is *not* there. There are no games, power-struggles, drama, anxiety, or anguish. No fakeness. No shocking unpleasant surprises.

We learn if we see those unsettling behaviors and feel those unsettling feelings, we are dealing with a still-infected person, someone who will eventually take our help without helping in return. Our bodies often know before our minds do. There may be a knot in our stomach, creepy or sinking sensation.

These reactions serve as a built-in alarm system telling us to get away quickly.

Day 65

With another person who is being restored by God's touch the bond forms gently over time. It grows through repeated contact in situations when first one of us has a practical need for a helpful act of cooperation, then the other needs something in return.

Hands-on, practical problem solving is what builds deep trusting friendships. Sharing a task reveals the other person's true competence and intent in a way that words alone can't.

We have learned that until we have shared a practical task from beginning to end multiple times with someone, it is unwise to form a long-term alliance as we really don't know who they are, only who they claim to be.

Day 66

The relationship with a new person you can trust and safely build a long-term productive alliance with will have signature behaviors that arise naturally and spontaneously:

The new companion shares the same highest goal you have, something God wants to see happen on earth.

The new companion knows and cares about your unique contribution to achieving the highest goal you both share.

The new companion stays up to date on your progress toward making your unique contribution just as you do with the status of their unique contribution.

Day 67

The bond with another person who is recovering naturally deepens as life happens. Life includes loss, setbacks, and suffering.

When you suffer a setback, your new companion is there for you and suffers with you. This cuts the sadness in half and accelerates your recovery.

Day 68

There are wonderful surprises and reversals in life, when problems resolve in ways we never could have anticipated, better than we could have hoped.

With someone who is recovering from the sickness of selfishness, when something goes well for you, your new companion celebrates with you. Having someone be truly happy for you, with no envy, doubles your joy and replenishes your motivation to keep going in the face of obstacles.

When God is honored between two people, the struggle to create new solutions may be hard, but it is not lonely. Rather there is an ever deepening, satisfying camaraderie.

Day 69

In life we spend time with our companions, and we spend time apart.

A true companion thinks about you and your honorable struggle when you are not around and seeks resources that might help.

A true companion defends your interest and reputation in your absence.

A true companion brings helpful discoveries to your attention without being asked.

A true companion promises to do something to assist your struggle, then does it well, completes it on time, and keeps you informed along the way, keeping unpleasant surprises to a minimum.

Day 70

There is continuity and discontinuity in life. Some things we need to let go of and others we need to keep working on because they have not been resolved.

A true companion remembers and returns to conversations you have had about what matters most to you.

A true companion monitors developments in the things that continue to matter to you, to see if you need anything. You do the same in return.

Day 71

There are things in life we simply can't do alone no matter how disciplined we are. It is at least a two-person job.

A true companion is genuinely honored to be asked to help and often offers to help unasked.

A true companion takes no offense when you ask for a little more, or an adjustment in the help offered so that it really does help.

You naturally do these same things in return, never wanting to break the chain of reciprocity.

Day 72

God delights in relationships that are equally helpful in both directions. Reciprocal benefit is the essence of justice, a wonder to behold and a joy to experience. Such a relationship is very different from what goes on among the still-infected, and that difference stands out.

It is the one difference that makes all the difference by making the most of every other difference.

Day 73

Social species survive cooperatively. While still infected with uncooperative selfishness humans are in the minority among social species, at odds with what has worked for millions of years. They live lawless lives and create lawlessness as a way of life.

In an unregenerate state humans build civilizations to create surpluses, not justice.

God does not delight in surpluses, because they create scarcity in one place in order to create abundance in another. Surpluses always create injustice somewhere for some part of God's creation.

Historically surpluses have most often been built on theft and forced inequality. Surpluses most often involve forcing uniformity on a natural environment once rich in diversity.

Day 74

Once we find ourselves living withing stable reciprocal relationships we are no longer part of an excluded minority group. We have achieved true inclusion. We are included and welcomed happily in life itself, because we bring no untimely, unnatural death with us.

No longer outlaws, in a regenerating state, we rejoin the majority of social species on earth. We use our amazing brains to help create equal abundance for every creature where it has been placed by life, every day, right where we have been placed, during the time we have been given on earth.

We are the earnest payment God is making on an entirely new and different civilization. We are proof of concept. Our lives offer more hope than any and all technologies combined.

Day 75

God does diversity by expecting and fostering mutually beneficial, helpful, cooperative relationship between people, and between humans and other species.

The cure for uncooperative selfishness does not produce selflessness.

Rather the cure restores what limits selfishness enough to keep open an untrammeled space between ourselves and other lives. That open space is safe enough that cooperative solutions can be worked out through productive disagreement and experimentation.

God pairs up individuals and groups who are deeply different from each other but can still work together to get things done on behalf of earth, things that would never happen otherwise.

Day 76

A bond which has formed between ethically recovering people is so productive and so rare, it is natural to protect it, maintain it and cultivate it just as we would anything else we cherish and identify with.

The natural bonds that grow between us form a lattice which becomes our real home, our place of safety and repair.

Consequently, we take more pride in, and better care of the lattice of relationships between us than we do any building or any house we might own. The reason is simple: our relationships are alive and evolving in response to our changing situation. Buildings and houses are not alive. They cannot grow or evolve by themselves.

Day 77

By working together in helpful, cooperative ways, our lives and our work continue to unfold in useful and interesting ways. We don't live tedious or repetitive lives, even though we accept tedious and repetitive tasks required to bring order to the situations we share.

When we try to advance inside systems controlled by the still infected – we find we can either have a life that is interesting, but not cooperative, or we can have a life that is cooperative but not interesting.

If it is interesting, it is because there is constant rivalry and conflict, which causes anger and anxiety. If it is cooperative, it is because of uniformity and groupthink, making life boring, predictable, and tedious.

Worst of all, we found we often ended up with a life that was neither interesting nor cooperative, especially in old age.

Day 78

While we were still in the grip of the infection, there came a time when we didn't sleep well.

Our deeply buried trait woke up and started to talk to us in the middle of the night- "there has to be more to life than this!"

We knew we were not fully alive inside. We somehow knew with powerful certainty this state of existence wasn't healthy or normal, much less optimal. We sensed that if this continued we would feel increasingly dead inside.

We saw the deadness in the faces of those around us.

Day 79

The helpful, cooperative trait can almost be called "the aliveness gene." It lights up and starts to take over when we start to get used to a zombie existence – not able to die, but not able to really live either.

We have learned through direct personal involvement that the zombie state is where unchecked selfishness leads, for individuals, families, and any larger organization we might attempt to form to solve our problems.

Alarmed, we called out to our Creator for help. We knew we didn't know the way out. God met us, helped us, and taught us about natural happiness and how to get there.

Day 80

When the aliveness trait turns on, it prompts us to reach for God, hungers to absorb the genius of nature and starts to change our attitudes and behaviors.

We are experiencing regeneration.

Regeneration is when a lost or missing adaptive faculty turns on and starts to function again, growing until it reaches full strength.

Somehow the disease of uncooperative selfishness arrests the natural development of the neural pathways that regulate empathy, creative intimacy, and conscience.

Regeneration restores these pathways.

Day 81

Humans have language and can pass on collective learning. Humans can make tools to extend the power of their senses and muscles. This combination allows us to develop vast and powerful creative capacities.

If our empathy remains stunted a gap grows between our capacities and our ability to wisely use those capacities. We end up like a car with an ever more powerful engine but ever weaker brakes and stiffer, more unresponsive steering.

Without regeneration, humanity is a tragic accident waiting to happen.

Under God's daily touch, our ethics start to catch up with our brainpower. This allows God's happiness to catch up with our choices, which allows kindness and honor to fill our most vital relationships to overflowing.

Day 82

Like an oasis in a vast desert, a striking contrast between two ways of living will stand out to anyone who is tired of what is out there and who aches to find something better.

Our lives provide that contrast - quietly, without self-promotion.

As an ethically recovering, but marginalized people, there are many things we must not do because accessing the resources and opportunities needed to do those things requires being indifferent or harmful to other lives.

But we find to our surprise there is one thing we can do that does not require access to more resources and opportunities. Unlike consumer products, what we produce is rare, exquisite, and valuable, but is still available to anyone, with or without lots of money.

Day 83

Under God's constant ethical guidance, we produce something quietly astonishing – a life that is at once both cooperative and interesting.

We don't live in constant fear of each other. We have no reason to.

We also have no reason to fear waking up to another meaningless, boring day filled with nothing but predictable producing, consuming, and quarreling.

There is nothing more interesting than participating in God's ongoing work of creation.

Day 84

As God meets us daily, teaches us and helps us to understand natural happiness and change, our daily behaviors come to differ dramatically from those of the sickened majority.

As a natural consequence the outcomes we produce over time are also dramatically different in quality and duration.

We don't purchase our interesting, rich way of living with money because it cannot be bought or sold using money.

Day 85

Like all other species that are still happily part of earth, we purchase our distinctly different, beautiful way of life with our own time, sustained attention, and problem-solving work.

Things that temporarily mask pain and elevate moods can be bought, sold, or hoarded. Access to them can be limited to those with money and power.

A way of living that makes us fully happy and keeps doing so can't work that way. Such a life can only be created freely together and then freely enjoyed together.

Day 86

This unique quality of life only emerges within and between small, intimate groups, all of whom are recovering from the sickness of uncooperative selfishness.

There was a time when we worked to be included in a society others created and controlled to benefit themselves, not life on earth.

Now that we have created something alive, something that is interesting and worthy, others work to secure a place for themselves in what we have created.

Day 87

Those who manage land are always on the lookout for invasive species that can wreak havoc on all the other species that live there.

Our new way of ethical living is not ours to change as we wish, any more than a thriving natural ecosystem is ours to alter any way we want. What we now enjoy was built under God's direction for divine purposes.

We have been trusted to keep it healthy and functional by protecting it from harm, so we must be very careful what we allow into the mix.

Day 88

We are also not allowed to stop change in its tracks. God designed us to constantly grow and change in response to our environment, both as individuals and as a group.

A good change creates more diversity. More diversity provides more options for life to move forward as the earth changes.

A bad change creates less diversity, as does refusing to change. Less diversity reduces the options life has to move forward as the earth changes and puts us all at risk of a slow decline into irrelevance, and eventual extinction.

The Creator will not assist us in stopping change or in introducing a change, if what we are attempting to harms the body of another creature or takes away the resources God provided so that creature could support itself.

Day 89

If a newcomer contributes something new within the ethical limits God has taught us, it will change us for the better. And change we must, if the newcomer brings observable facts and logic to the table we had not considered and shows us what we can do differently to brings us closer to God. We are open and hospitable. At any moment God could use a newcomer to help the way we cooperate more closely resemble the thriving, diverse systems we see in nature.

The newcomer was attracted by the vitality of our shared life, by the growing stock of happiness we all contribute to daily.

By receiving the newcomer's factual feedback and putting it to use, we become attractive to those who could not have seen the beauty in our way of living without the correction or addition the newcomer brought.

Healthy diversity attracts more of itself.

Day 90

God does change using the attractive power of growing, social momentum, not through clever marketing.

Our reputation precedes us, creating interest and openings. We are being regenerated and restored to God's natural purpose for humanity precisely so that we can grow, change, and attract newcomers, who will enrich and enliven our shared life even more.

Everything hinges on how we accept and include newcomers. That process is yet another thing that is distinctly different about us.

Day 91

In nature, form follows function. If something is beautiful, it also does something necessary and useful. Beauty is a natural side effect of good engineering. It is not merely painted on at the end of the process for decoration.

A good, healthy, productive, functioning social system will produce its own unique and beautiful forms, without conscious effort. Among us there is no drive to put on elaborate shows patterned after shows others put on elsewhere at another place or time.

Compared to justice and diversity, shows are easy and cheap to produce.

Civilization to date has produced plenty of shows, but far too little justice and almost no ability to manage diversity the way nature does.

We leave showmanship to the still-infected and turn our attention to what God wants most for life on earth.

Day 92

In nature, beauty evokes desire. Others long to share in the well-being they see among us. What attracts newcomers is the peaceful beauty and efficient contentment of our lives, without the stench of complacency, smugness, or self-righteousness.

We have not arrived. We are in transit and could lose our way at any point. We must remain fully engaged and aware of our situation to see its pitfalls and its potential.

Our shared life is both energized by creative tension and stable enough to incubate new, different, better ways of doing what we must do to live long and happily.

Day 93

Drawn to the growing well-being they see among us, the newcomer starts to offer something good and useful in hopes we will value it enough to include it in what we are doing.

Since we have been entrusted with protecting and sustaining what God directed us to create, we can't just say yes to any offers we receive.

At the same time, we know how painful it is to offer the best we have and have it rejected, because that is what the majority did to us. There is no deeper rejection.

So instead of saying yes to any and all offers, we say...

"Yes, if... yes, as long as...."

Day 94

Our acceptance is conditional. It is contingent upon meeting high ethical standards.

Upholding standards of excellence increases our standing in the eyes of a newcomer. We are not needy and desperate. We know they need us more than we need them. We will live full and productive lives without them if necessary. The reverse cannot be said, and they know it.

Unconditional acceptance flatters the newcomer, which stops all growth. Conditional acceptance pays a deep compliment to newcomers. It says we believe in their capacity to grow into all they can be, to overcome whatever stands between them and God's delight.

We fully expect them to do so, without exception.

Day 95

We expect constant lifetime growth into full maturity from anyone who lives among us, none more than those we entrust with leadership, whose decisions affect all of us for years to come.

If we see leadership talent in the newcomer we are even more vigilant in upholding our highest values - God's purposes for life as far as we understand them to date.

Day 96

We require that any newcomer interact with us and carry out any tasks we need done within the ethical limits that allow us to keep trusting each other so we can be helpful and cooperative.

A newcomer can start by doing a task we need done well, on time, in a way that enhances what we are doing. We will learn more about a newcomer by doing work with them for an hour, than we would in a year of conversation with them.

In the meantime, the newcomer needs to unlearn and abandon the certainties they brought with them about happiness and how change happens, as they start to learn how to seek and know God directly.

It will take time and struggle for a newcomer to establish a stable ethical connection to their Creator informed by a deep respect for the genius in creation.

Day 97

When newcomers are recovering from the sickness, there are moments when the struggle feels hopeless. The temptation to defect and go back to the lies is very strong. Yet they won't want to give up the benefits of living among us.

Since we tried it ourselves, we know what they will try.

Early in their recovery they will try to stay among us, but reintroduce the lies that lead to selfish, unhelpful, uncooperative behavior, just sure there is an easier way than the way we do things. They suggest that all we must do to make things easier is overlook an ethical lapse.

All it takes is one person looking to take advantage of others' helpfulness to destabilize our relationships and cause us to quickly feel unsafe when we are working together on something.

Day 98

If one of us starts to win at the expense of another, or at the expense of all of us, we start to lose our ability to collaborate. We start to hold back, to give less of what we could give, now that there is a good chance it will be taken and nothing of substance given in return.

The less we each contribute, the cheaper the contribution each of us makes, the harder and more unpleasant it becomes to create new and better solutions to the problems we face together in our situation. Once unlimited selfishness enters the mix again, both the process and the outcomes will no longer bear the fingerprints of God.

Day 99

A culture of cooperation is elegant, but it is not invulnerable. To think it will always be there no matter how we treat it is the very attitude that has led to the near ruin of the earth.

We can't allow ideas that authorize selfish cheating to take root again among us. It does not matter how attractively packaged the ideas are, or how ancient or prestigious the pedigree of the clever idea, or how much quicker and easier its solutions to our challenges promise to be.

The idea that "quick and easy" is a goal worth pursuing is one lie that is sure to set loose the disease among us.

Day 100

There are moments of creative breakthrough that come naturally out of our problem-solving struggles when we find a much more efficient solution than the one we have been trying.

In nature there are ingenious solutions that use the least energy possible to get the best result possible. We keep an eye out for those efficiencies, but ease is not what we pursue because ease is not our standard, justice is our standard.

Effort-saving efficiencies *ensue* naturally as a by-product of *pursuing* justice – the highest well-being possible for all the lives entrusted to our care.

Day 101

As founders of a new sustainable civilization, it is our duty to build social systems that are a joy to manage and administer. It would be unjust of us to construct something that would be a nightmare to operate and maintain for those who follow us.

To avoid this, we seek the counsel of those among us gifted at managing honorably, who know how to create on-going cooperative endeavors characterized by high performance and high fulfillment.

A gifted manager will spot a problem we may not see at first: A cheap short cut today, used to avoid the challenging task of addressing cheating behavior, usually makes operating the system harder if not impossible in the future. Worse, it sets a precedent of laziness and cowardice.

We are very sensitive to the precedents we set. We cry out to God and seek a better way. We are prepared to put in more time and effort so that those who follow us can put their energy into what comes next, rather than constantly fixing what we should have built better to begin with.

We daily receive God's best. In return we owe God nothing less than our best.

Day 102

The reason we can't allow cheating to go on unaddressed is simple. The cheater, the loafer, the schemer, the bully, the one who takes from the social system and gives nothing back – will appear to "win" and make those of us who honor God's priorities look like naïve "losers" to the impatient eye.

Early in our recovery from the sickness, we constantly wobble between trusting God, who is invisible and Whom we cannot control, and trusting something other than God which is visible that humans can control.

Having a cynical, untrusting "winner" around would be like trying to recover from addiction while spending time with someone who is still using the drug.

Day 103

As soon as cheating behavior shows up we know we must deal with it. We knew it would happen. How we deal with cheating behavior among us reveals that God really has changed us, or that it was all just empty words all along.

Cheating behavior must change into cooperative behavior.

God affects change in us and through us, using the messy details of the challenge the way an athletic trainer uses the student's own body weight to build muscle groups. Difficulties cause growth when we face and address them when and where they appear in our lives.

Day 104

Cheating behavior is to our social lives what cancer is to our bodies. Cancer is so difficult to cure because it uses the processes of life itself – against life. Cancer is the only thing in nature that never pauses in its growth. Cancer is smart and figures out a way to overcome anything thrown at it.

To cure uncooperative selfishness God does not ask us to become selfless. That is neither possible nor desirable. Every living thing must maintain and grow itself using the resources it finds in its environment before it can contribute to a cooperative effort.

Day 105

We don't want anyone to lose the vital energy of life, to become limp and passive. People in that condition may be easier to control, but they are useless, and even dangerous in times of crisis.

The way to deal with the problems of strength is not to make us weak, but rather to learn how to make the most productive use of all our strengths.

Each of us must have a strong, decisive, skilled, determined self to have anything valuable to contribute to a strong, decisive, skilled, determined group as it solves problems larger than anyone can solve alone.

Day 106

There are deep, legitimate, and necessary differences between us, even when we are recovering from the disease. Our interests and needs are often not the same and are sometimes at odds. Our past experiences give us different points of view, each of which provides useful information for problem-solving.

Our differences are legitimate. Yet there are remnants of the disease in all of us, ready to grow again, wanting to throw off all limits on our own selfishness while limiting the selfishness of others, all in the name of God. The problem lies not in their being differences between us, but in how to manage them honorably and productively to benefit all of us.

We sense immediately we are in over our heads when we find ourselves in conflict. We know everything is at stake. Instinctively and immediately, we call out to God.

Day 107

As always, God answers our call. Under God's ethical guidance, we resolve differences into a new, higher order of cooperation. We forge our most significant new cooperative structures in the furnace of our own internal disagreements and disputes.

Among us, both sides of a conflict emerge in a different, higher state than before the conflict appeared. Both are closer to God and behave with more graceful precision than before, creating a social system that more closely resembles the elegant cooperative systems we see in nature.

Both sides emerge with a stronger patient eye.

Day 108

We learn first-hand that the long-term benefits of cooperation accrue and eventually exceed those of meeting our own needs at the expense of others and the effectiveness of the group. It will take a while for a newcomer to have enough positive experiences with the work of cooperation to see this pattern.

Only surprising, unforeseen firsthand experiences have the power to change human values for good.

Until then, we cling to the values we learned as children despite all the evidence that they have not served our individual or shared interests very well for very long.

Day 109

We have learned that we suffer less in the long run if we address problems between us regularly as soon as they appear. By making regular investments in increased, peaceful complexity we find we have enough time and energy to meet the challenge.

We don't wait for a more convenient time because there never will be one.

If we put off the work of conflict resolution the issues between us pile up and combine. Eventually the conflict grows beyond our available time and energy to deal with it.

Day 110

Through hard experience we have discovered that unresolved disagreements inevitably become disputes. At least one party has taken a loss, places blame on the other and demands restitution.

The second party refuses to take the blame and instead places it the first party in return. It is at these impasses societies break apart. Under God's prompting and guidance, we don't allow this to happen. We put out fires when they are small and then build a structure out of new values that are less combustible to begin with.

In so doing we find the constant exercise of effective, honorable conflict resolution prepares us to quickly adapt to substantial changes in our situation, whether they are dangerous or promising.

Day 111

Musicians know, the more you practice, the better you can improvise. Conflict resolution opens new pathways of creativity and trains the muscles of the soul for quick, precise response.

Constantly re-solving the conflicts that come from being different, as soon as they show up, serves the same function for a group that the liver serves for the body, removing toxins before they can do harm, especially to the brain.

The ancients thought the liver was the seat of human courage. It does take courage to enter and resolve conflict as an ongoing, normal practice.

Day 112

Practicing courage is essential, as courage does not just magically appear when needed. If we have not been using the courage we have, we lose it. If we use what courage we have in situations that require it, we gain more.

We can't ship up real, reliable courage quickly through cheerleading. Rather, courage is like a muscle; we must use however much we can summon when the situation requires it or lose it.

We build functional courage slowly, by applying new values and disciplines when needed to surmount real threats to our ethic of cooperation.

Day 113

We begin the process of conflict resolution differently. What makes us different is where we look for solutions to the problems that arise from sharing a space at the same time, while not having identical goals.

In aviation, "attitude control" is knowing where the airplane is pointed at all times.

There is nothing more important than attitude control.

When we are in any kind of danger, especially the danger of internal conflict, the first thing we do is direct our attention to something different than we did when we were still sickened.

We keep our attention focused in a very particular direction all the way through the process of problem-solving and creative conflict resolution.

Day 114

Up in the air, everything is fluid. Without the ground to support it, the position of an airplane changes constantly, in three dimensions. To properly orient and control the plane the pilot must always know where the horizon is and the position of the plane in relationship to it, for a simple reason.

The horizon is the one thing that does not change.

The horizon marks the limit of what we can see, yet that limit itself is constant and dependable. Only by focusing on what does not change can we solve the problems that arise from constant change in everything else.

Day 115

When we work our way through the fog of our internal struggles we don't look for final direction to anything that changes, no matter how fast or slow it changes. To settle a question and move to action...

We don't look across the sea for how an older, foreign, esteemed culture does things.

We don't look across the land to see how our own native culture does things.

We don't look to the past to how our ancestors did things.

We don't look to an imagined future, to a utopia in which people use amazing recent technology, while being just as selfish as they are now.

We don't look in books, old or new. We don't look to the press, popular gurus, or movements. We don't look to what everyone else is doing.

We don't look to ourselves, to feel and imagine what we really, really want.

These sources can help prepare our minds to spot a new solution, but they are not a sure guide to action.

All familiar human solutions to our current challenges fail due to two changing features of reality. 1) Messy details and 2) Constant change in the mix of messy details.

Day 116

Our situation is novel. Our exact combination of local variables has never occurred before and will never occur again. In addition, our situation keeps changing so any understanding we gain is provisional at best.

So where do we look? What do we look to? What do we look at?

We look to God. Alone. In solitude. In nature. God is our Creator. We listen for God's gentle voice in silence as we look for God's genius in Creation, surrounded by the richness and wisdom embedded in life.

No one can do this for us. No one can package this experience for us. We feel alone but we are alone with God. There is no better place to be.

Day 117

We see the horizon - the limits to our certainty and control.

Humbly, alone with our Creator, we acknowledge God's unlimited knowledge and wisdom and remember that will never change. God will always be beyond us, no matter how much we learn. God will always know what is best for all of life, no matter what unforeseen events occur.

We recommit to staying so close to God, so available to God, that we can feel the slightest hint of an ethical lapse, at the very beginning of an idea that involves throwing off limits to our selfishness.

Day 118

As we work through the lengthy process of resolving a conflict between us, we ask for and receive constant guidance every step of the way. We seek God before and after every conversation that touches on the conflict.

When we are unsure what course of action would honor God, we stop, we call out to God, we wait, watch, and listen. Sometimes the only thing that is clear is that it is not yet clear what to do.

Nothing is wrong. We have done nothing wrong. When scientists conduct an experiment and discover nothing new, that is itself considered a finding.

We pause. We sleep on it. God does not leave us in the lurch. On the rare occasion when something needs to be done right now, we find we always have enough ethical clarity to avoid doing harm, at the very least. This keeps open the possibility of a new, better solution.

Day 119

As we patiently and carefully work our way through the conflicts that come from diversity, what to do next and how to do it becomes clearer through action and feedback, if we promptly respond positively to the guidance we receive.

All those other sources of guidance come into play in a most surprising way. They were place holders. They promised a solution to come but could not deliver the solution.

Often in beautiful verse and song, the best insights from the past sustained our hope and focused our attention until we saw the opening God created. In that opening God begins a new work on earth.

Day 120

The inspiring promises and placeholders from the past can never replace intimate contact with the infinite mind of God. Rather, these written statements serve to keep us seeking intimate, learning, growing contact with God, nature, and each other.

When God brings us to a new insight, our own local, timely, original, creative, courageous actions are what turn into reality what could once we could only imagine and hope for.

Like the experience of learning to ride a bike by using training wheels for a while, we borrow the wisdom of written statements until our own wisdom can take over.

There comes a moment when our own experiences and memories provide more precise more guiding information than the written statements we started with.

Day 121

We must never squander an opening from God. Once we have enough ethical clarity to take responsible action, delayed response becomes non-response and cuts off the flow of divine guidance.

Delayed response stops the cycle of action, feedback and learning upon which all natural innovation is based.

We can't presume divine guidance will start flowing again whenever it is convenient for us. Humans seek God on God's terms and on God's schedule. God does not wait on any human or human group but moves on to those who stay receptive and responsive.

Day 122

The Creator embedded infinite intelligence in creation. Creation has been doing what it does for billions of years, long before our species existed and will keep doing it long after we are gone.

Creation has its own God-given way of doing things. We humans, as individuals, as a civilization, as a species, are too small and temporary to alter the forces and processes of creation. We are free to choose our actions, but not the consequences of our actions.

Those larger, older forces and processes will always determine the consequences of our actions.

Day 123

We don't ask God to adjust the forces of reality to us. We don't try to make God adjust reality to our wishes. It can't be done. We aren't here to adjust reality to suit us because reality isn't about us and doesn't revolve around us.

We can't possibly know what is best for all of life or where it is all heading.

Instead, we are the ones who do whatever it takes to adjust to God's way of doing things. God's way of doing things works with the way creation does things.

Day 124

We work to understand as much as we can in a lifetime how God does things, as captured in the amazing processes of life.

From there we alter our expectations and actions so that they protect, enhance, and extend what God is already doing, as best as we can tell. Anything we do is always open to correction and redirection from God.

Life already has a way and is under way using it. Peace, contentment, and fruitfulness only come from going life's way.

Day 125

When we realize we have been trying to force our will on God or creation, we stop. We acknowledge our foolishness and pride. We know we have disconnected our souls from divine guidance and protection. We feel the pain of remorse and acknowledge our errors to God. God mercifully responds and connects us again to the constant signal of ethical, creative guidance.

God is the God of new beginnings. Just as God brought life to a once lifeless planet, God brings the wonder of adaptive, changing, growing life back into our own lives. We are once again moving along by God's side. We now take God's side in any situation which affects the well-being and potential of other lives.

Day 126

While we were still infected with unlimited selfishness we were proud. We had a false sense of proportion and significance. We thought it was all about us and revolved around us, which produced hardness in our hearts and harshness in our words and actions.

Our hard harshness had a hardening effect on others and made them harsher.

Day 127

If we are recovering from the disease of unlimited selfishness we will feel regret after being hard and harsh toward others, especially if they have been helpful to us.

The experience of remorse and return is healing and leaves our hearts warm and tender. We are far more compassionate and patient with others than we were before. We realize faster when we are about to act in a way that is contrary to life's way and stop. We wait until we know how to proceed in a way that honors God.

This waiting is not delayed response; it is our timely response to God. It takes humility to wait on One greater than our selves.

Day 128

Humility comes from seeing reality as it is. It involves having an accurate sense of proportion and significance when it comes to our place in it all, no more and no less than can be demonstrated factually.

Remorse and return experiences make us humbler than we were before, which produces a natural gentleness.

Our gentleness has a gentling effect on others.

Day 129

In nature, where there is diversity there is tension and competition, but it all functions as an integrated whole. Overall, there is a harmony that is more gentle than not. Within a system of gentle harmony, when there is conflict we expect to see it resolve quickly, and it usually does, often at a higher level of complexity.

Within a harsh social environment, we don't expect to see conflicts resolved quickly or at all, and they usually only get worse.

Day 130

Climate is what we expect to experience. Weather is what we do experience on any given day. We stock our closets based on what we expect to experience during the season, then adjust what we choose to wear each day based on the weather. Something similar happens with our social behaviors.

If we expect selfish behavior, we stock selfish or spiteful behavior to use in return. We tend to see what we expected to see and do what we have prepared ourselves to do. On the other hand, if we expect to see helpful, cooperative behavior, we stock helpful and cooperative behaviors to use in return.

As we experience the regeneration of our souls, the effect we have is to change the social climate from harshness to gentleness. This changes the prospects and probabilities for life around us, and ultimately for life's future on earth.

By seeking and following God's daily ethical guidance, we turn vicious cycles into virtuous ones.

Day 131

There is a delayed response to God's ethical promptings that is essentially saying "no" to God. It is not confusion. It is refusal. Willful refusal severs the stable connection that carries the signal of wise, creative direction.

We learn nothing turns out well after saying no to God. So, we say yes to God, even during the confusion and worry we feel in the midst of a conflict. We know God has not abandoned us just because it is not yet clear what to do.

We maintain attitude control at all costs. We trust, listen, watch until a solution unfolds that is honorable and deepens our trust in God, our admiration for nature, and our ability to work together.

Day 132

There is also a sneaky kind of delayed response. It is not brazenly saying no to God, but rather saying, "no, not right now. I have something important to do first. I will get to that when I can." We promptly put God's requirement at the bottom of our to do list.

It is the first thing dismissed under stress and the last thing attended to, once we are rested, if nothing else comes up.

This kind of delayed response to God tells us something is very wrong that must be corrected in our hearts. It signals that we think we are the center of the universe, that everything is about us and our own goals, which once secured, will make us happy in a way that God can't.

Day 133

The reason we delay response to God's promptings is we are busy responding to something else we deem to be more important.

We all enter the process of regeneration riddled with attachments to things that we are just sure will make us happy. When one of those things, people, or experiences becomes available or is threatened our entire nervous system lights up and becomes highly agitated.

This agitation clogs our connection to God and stops the flow of ethical creative guidance.

Our moment of guided action passes and all the good that could have happened is lost. Within hours of being disrespectful to God we find ourselves being disrespectful to others. They respond in kind. As a result, our world becomes a place that makes us even more agitated, and the cycle begins again.

Day 134

In an agitated state we can't hear the quiet voice of God or feel the gentle touch redirecting our concern and attention. In an agitated state nature can seem completely irrelevant and even boring.

Before we can become truly available to God we must enter God's change process, which systematically removes all those attachments until one day we realize we can encounter a stimulus that once would have set off in us a storm or anxiety, greed, or envy, and instead we now feel nothing at all. Under God's touch we have changed and grown.

Day 135

God removes our distracting attachments by using our brain's natural plasticity. Like everything God makes, the brain is very efficient and does not waste energy.

Without being told to do so, our brains automatically prune away neuropathways it registers we won't be using anymore and naturally grows the neuropathways we clearly are going to be using constantly. What we use grows and what we don't use we lose.

Day 136

Without our daily time in quiet communion with God, using nature as our curriculum, this natural pruning does not happen.

When we do maintain our daily quiet, uninterrupted time with God, our attention is refocused, and the pruning continues gently, until one day, after years of practice, we realize we have forgotten things that used to cause agitation.

The things that once agitated our souls simply aren't there anymore or they aren't strong enough to hurl us around the way they used to.

Day 137

Over time God redirects our attention and uses brain plasticity to replace thought patterns we got from our culture with thought patterns that track with the way life solves problems in nature.

We become very different from the culture around us. Something greater, something more powerful controls our souls now.

We feel a wonderful freedom. We are freed from what used to distress us, which frees us for our task of being useful to God and helpful to life.

Day 138

As God changes what commands our attention and concern, we become available to God's quiet direction in a way that we were not before.

We see results from our guided actions which we did not see before. Like a healthy garden, the work of our hands may be small, but it is real and alive. We see a shared well-being form that develops, adjusts, and changes itself as needed, the way all livings do.

Fruitful activity is deeply rewarding. Feeling rewarded reinforces the new neural pathways, making us even more eagerly available to God.

We feel we are an essential part of the new shared well-being, but we know it does not revolve around us, it revolves around the certainty that God is present among us as long as we create and protect justice between the lives around us.

Day 139

It takes years of receiving God's guidance, but where there was once a vicious cycle of upsetting thoughts, feelings, and behaviors, there emerges a virtuous cycle of constructive thoughts, feelings, and behaviors.

The more we focus on things that are helpful and true, the more those things become real to us. In so doing, since we can't focus on two things at once, the less we focus on things that are unhelpful and false, those things dim, fade, and lose their power over us.

We simply forget to upset ourselves and others the way we used to.

Forgetting is so freeing, it feels like a miracle...and it is.

Day 140

As God changes us from the inside out we become increasingly alive to God and what God is doing in nature and increasingly dead to what would distract us from our intended role in it all.

We have learned to be intimately receptive and responsive to God and what only God can do. We no longer break ranks with God to chase something "better" because we know there is nothing better.

The only realistic way to do this is to become unreceptive and unresponsive to the latest big projects of powerful humans who want our help to become more powerful; projects which at best come to nothing, but which usually end up doing more harm than good.

We have learned that God does no work that results in nothing and only supports work that will bring a widely shared well-being to earth, so that is where we direct our time and attention.

Day 141

God will always be very active in the process of creating justice and peace. God will always be involved in helping us manage and cultivate the diversity we find among us and around us.

This is why we go to so much trouble to resolve our conflicts differently than the culture around us.

Bringing peace out of diversity is the work in which we can be most sure to be met, taught, and helped by God.

Day 142

What sets our new civilization apart from the one God calls us to replace is the way we approach the distribution of information and power. If we don't make this change, we will never be able to cultivate and optimize the diversity that God so clearly loves.

The defining feature of all past city-based civilizations has been a way of organizing that gives ever fewer people the power to control ever more people, and to control and use ever more parts of their lives to enrich the few at the top.

In all previous civilizations there was always very little if any diversity at the top and they liked it that way. Without diversity at the top the decisions made there always harm diversity farther down from the top and farther out from the center.

Day 143

In all prior city-based civilizations, the few at the top prospered at the expense of the many below them.

It all started with a monopoly on knowledge.

If only the few can access the knowledge needed to solve our shared problems, the few will rule everyone else. Those at the top have unwritten rules that govern how things happen. They only share their unwritten rules with those who look like themselves and promise to keep them in power.

Day 144

God delights in breaking up monopolies.

It is liberating to realize the knowledge we need to solve our shared problems is everywhere, in every situation and accessible to everyone always.

To our amazement, we find we already have the information and insight we need to rule ourselves wherever we find ourselves in space and time. This means God can rule wherever we are in any situation we find ourselves.

Day 145

All along God intended for all of us to have knowledge, freedom, and self-reliance so we could enjoy independence, dignity, and unity as we serve God's purposes on earth.

Without direct, constant access to the knowledge we need, we give up those precious gifts in exchange for the false security of stuff. It is a bad trade.

To find the information we need to make good decisions, we look to God, listen to our conscience, carefully learn from nature, and check the record of those who have dealt with similar issues in the past to see what worked and what didn't.

The answers we need were there all along, waiting for us to find, process and combine them. We never needed the monopoly to begin with. As a liberated people we are no longer stuck with the costly errors monopolies always produce.

Day 146

The few at the top of the current order cannot stop us from seeking God, listening to our conscience, making our own historical records, or observing nature.

We are free to make our own decisions and solve our own problems in ways that don't benefit the far away few, but rather, benefit ourselves and those we love right where we are, without hurting any other life with whom we share a space.

Under God's direction we build a society designed primarily to create justice – to ensure all forms of life have what they need to become all God intended them to be.

Day 147

As for material means, God designed our new civilization from the ground up to create justice that fosters excellence, not luxury that causes waste.

God is the master of logistics, making sure each creature has what it needs, where it needs it, when it needs it, for as long as it needs it, then recycling resources to get them to the next creature who needs them.

God's happiness is built on just enough, just in time.

It is not our place to disturb God's logistics.

Day 148

We learn that repairing the damage caused by a system built to create surplus instead of justice is not doing a work of justice worthy of God.

Remediating harm, though noble and necessary, is a lower order of work than creating real justice in the first place. Creating real justice causes no harm needing remediation.

Remediating is a lower order of work because of the waste. By the time a justice system finally remediates harm entire lives or ecosystems have been irreparably ruined.

God expects better of us and gave us big brains so we could do better than just clean up preventable messes repeatedly.

Day 149

Constantly remediating harm caused by the godless only emboldens them, because they learn someone else will try to clean up their mess.

At the point of despair and exhaustion, we come to see that we are perpetuating the harm by eliminating the cost those doing it would otherwise have to bear themselves.

There comes a time when God directs us away from necessary and compassionate repair work to the work of founding something new, something entirely different.

God has called us be founders of a new civilization.

As founders we learned the values we hold most dear from the painful experience of trying to repair systems that never could stay fixed, because their creators never designed them to embody God's way of doing things.

Day 150

The beginning of a new civilization is not a building or engineering project. The beginning of a new civilization is memory, a mental map of what not to do and what to do, and why.

We are determined not to repeat the mistakes that led to an unjust society and devasted planet. God directs us to wipe the slate clean, start over, and learn the deeper lessons of life.

Life already has a way and is underway using it. We are determined to learn life's ways of solving problems and build those lessons into everything we create.

Day 151

In our new civilization the "justice system" will not exist primarily to repair harm already done, but rather to resolve honest disagreements between us. We will passionately disagree at times. There will often be different options to create justice for all life, everywhere, with what we have available at the moment.

God has designed our new justice system to prevent harm before it happens, so we put our effort into resolving disagreements between us about what to do next.

Day 152

We find the more effectively we resolve disagreements about what to do in the future, the less we must deal with disputes about who is to blame for something that happened in the past.

History teaches us that the winners soon forget, but the losers never do and will wait for centuries if necessary to get revenge.

We are determined to create a society that does not produce losers in the first place, especially those whose losses fund the privileges of the winners.

We struggle to create peace ahead of time, so we don't have to spend so much effort trying to restore peace afterwards.

Day 153

It is the way of nature to prevent wasting a pound of cure for a disorder by investing an ounce of prevention as early as possible.

Life is difficult. We don't have a choice not to struggle. We only have a choice of what kind of struggle to engage in.

There are struggles that lead to death and extinction. There are struggles that lead to more life and life at a higher level of complexity and beauty. We choose to embrace and optimize the struggles that come with sharing a space while being different. We choose adaptive struggle, which is the ounce of prevention.

Day 154

Nature uses the process of adaptive struggle to harness diversity and turn it into synergy. Synergy is a dynamic, moving whole that is more than the sum of its parts. The interaction patterns that form between parts are themselves new parts of the whole.

When we are creating new and better interactions between ourselves we are creating what God creates the way God creates.

Productive synergy is the standard God expects us to work toward as we resolve the conflicts that arise between us.

Day 155

If I don't let the few at the top of the current, dying civilization control how I relate to God, I have an open space in which new patterns of interaction can be conceived and grow. My solitude becomes a cherished meeting place between myself and my Creator where original work gets done.

In the silence of that open space, informed by nature's patterns, I hear a gentle, quiet voice. There is a nudge toward a way to resolve our conflict that I never thought of before, one that promotes and sustains creative synergy, making the most of our differences.

Day 156

If I don't let the few at the top control how I relate to my life partner, we leave an open space between us in which new, peaceful solutions can be born, take root and grow. Together we feel the guiding intelligence of God, directing our attention and effort toward a higher form of cooperation.

As long as we don't let the few at the top control how we manage the quietness of our living space, as long as we refuse to let the powerful fill our house, our minds, our conversations with their ideas, values, language, and drama, we have reserved an open space in which something better can emerge.

By reserving a space for our Most Honored Guest, we ensure God will visit us often. God's visits happen in our own minds and within our closest relationships.

Day 157

Looking into each other's eyes provides more useful information than looking at screens filled with images of people who can't look back into our own eyes.

I can see immediately how what I just said or did falls on my partner and immediately adjust my actions to make sure we can maintain a just peace between us. One-on-one, in private, my partner can do the same. We see immediately whether we have created a moment of justice or injustice between us. The more moments of justice we create, the more often we experience surprise visits from God.

In this way we prevent unresolved conflicts from building up between us.

Drama is the sudden release of the built-up energy of unresolved conflict. Peace is the steady flow of creative energy to solve the problems of a shared life in new and better ways. The more peaceful we become, the more we see the value in all the ways our differences enrich our lives.

Day 158

If we don't let the few at the top don't control everything about how we produce and what we consume, we leave an open space where we can work out new ways of producing and consuming that are good for us and the earth.

No one can force us to gain all our safety and comfort at the expense of the misery of other living things, so we don't do it.

At every small, intimate opportunity, we create a quiet and growing rebellion. We refuse to go along just to get along. We deny an unjust system our attention, admiration, and energy.

We simply walk away and do something new, different, and better, right where we are, with the resources we already have in hand.

Day 159

We have learned that the composition of God's wellbeing is about 70% what we don't allow to happen that previous civilizations did allow. It is about 30% about things we insist must happen that previous civilizations didn't insist upon. It is what we don't do that creates an open space for God's peace to enter and rule within and among us.

We don't wait for a mystical, magical semi-divine human to arrive and solve our problems.

We don't need or seek anyone's attention or permission.

We don't need or seek followers. We seek to follow God.

We don't need others to like us. We need to be like God.

We may use technology, but we don't expect gadgets to bring ethical force to bear in our situation.

We are determined that everything we do repeatedly to sustain and advance our happiness will come to embody God's genius as we see it embedded in nature. That starts with abandoning values and behaviors that are contrary to life's way of solving problems.

Day 160

We, the freed ones, the recovering ones, are the incubators of a new world.

In nature, incubators are small and hidden away from view.

Here, the seeds of a new world grow in the free, unexploited, unmonitored and unmonetized spaces we have created in our minds, our relationships, and our homes.

We are habitat for the future, one in which God will directly teach and rule every citizen's heart. In God's future for earth there will be little need for human hierarchy of any kind because people regulate their own behaviors. There will be no place for human authority that does not earn the right to lead both ethically and practically, every day.

Under these conditions we can build a future that benefits all lives everywhere equally.

Day 161

We have learned to cooperate with God, not as equals, but happily subordinate to an Infinite Mind. We have learned to cooperate with each other, as equals before God, to create justice.

God intended each of us to be able to meet a particular need as well as the more general needs we all share.

We do justice to God's intention by acknowledging who is equal capable of meeting what need gift, training, and experience, while expecting everyone to contribute their share to the common good.

It does injustice to God's intention to treat everyone as equal to every task, because it is clearly not the case.

It is unjust to give the same weight to the counsel of those who have invested the most of themselves in our shared well-being as we give the counsel of those who have carefully avoided putting themselves at risk on our behalf.

Day 162

God manages equality differently, by calling and equipping some to someday be equal to one task and others to be equal to another task. From task to task, not every opinion from every member of our group is equal in value.

Most of the time the opinion of someone who has spent decades trying to understand how to solve a difficult problem and who has tried various solutions is not equal in value to the opinion of someone who has not done so.

Yet on rare occasions a newcomer sees the problem in a new light. God distributes insight and ability in surprising ways, so we stay on the lookout for a divine surprise from any quarter.

Day 163

Fresh insight can come from someone who naturally sees things differently, sees things we don't see, or sees clearly that we can only vaguely sense is going on. They were born this way and don't remember learning how to see what they see the way they see it.

What allows them to see these things may be a structural difference in their brains, provided by evolution for the advancement of the species. We don't fear the emergence of what life is doing next. Harm to our cherished notions is not harm to our bodies or means, so we welcome natural divergence.

In nature "more" means more differences, not more of the same.

More of the same as a means of increase is unsustainable.

More differences as a means of increase is sustainable because it provides life with options it may need when the environment around it changes, which it surely will do.

Day 164

We interact with each other in such a way that recognizes the value in one's deep insight and experience and recognizes the value in the fresh point of view, not one at the expense of the other.

Among the those who are regenerate, who are becoming wise, the veteran is courteous and open to the novice, and the novice respects the work invested by the veteran. The regenerating novice knows to not value labor is to discourage people from working hard for years on something if necessary.

The novice may well someday be in the same position as the veteran, so it is in the interest of the novice to uphold the culture of giving credit where credit is due.

Day 165

For each challenge, we discern those among us whom God has clearly equipped to take the lead on the task at hand, then follow their lead. Our leaders are not bullies or autocrats. Our leaders host and facilitate effective problem-solving sessions.

Trusting and following those among us who demonstrate the greatest skill at meeting the challenge at hand is a natural form of cooperation God built into all species that live in groups. This form of cooperation in particular functions to secure a group's survival into the future as its environment changes.

We reserve the greater honor for those who have clearly made the rarer and more costly contribution.

Day 166

Where none of us has any more gift or experience than any other we distribute the tasks and work together, each of us applying equal time and effort to figure out the most fitting solution.

We don't allow social loafing, which is when an individual benefits from the work of others but does not contribute anything of substance back to the group's effort. Social loafing comes from the assumption that "someone else will take care of that," when we see a task that needs to be done to keep things running or moving forward.

Social loafing is a sneaky, lingering symptom of the disease of unlimited selfishness. It is unjust to reward an entire group for an achievement produced mostly by one or two people, or to allow one member to take credit for the work of another or of an entire group.

How we treat our most committed and productive members foretells how we will treat any of our members. To the degree that we treat any member unjustly and don't correct it, we lose contact with God and forfeit divine direction, provision, and protection.

Confronting social loafing as soon as it appears is a natural form of social immune response, just as the body deals with pathogens as soon as it detects them. This is one of the most difficult conflicts to address but we have no choice.

Day 167

We willingly walk away from what is ruled unjustly and keep walking deeper into the rule of God. We are creating justice when we keep learning more about how to cooperate with the rest of nature, so we can survive and thrive together.

We did not need to be forced, threatened, bribed, lulled, flattered, or tricked into this new way of living.

We see this path as the better choice because it alone opens our lives to the fascinating genius of continuous creation.

Based on patient observation, facts, and logic, and motivated by love, admiration, and gratitude, we chose freely to unlearn all that not helpful, all that is uncooperative and too selfish to keep open a space for new solutions to emerge.

Day 168

We chose freely to participate in God's purposes, to help each other, and to contribute our individual resources to our shared well-being. Wonders await us around every corner.

God is the God of freedom.

God delights in those who freely choose to trust and follow a mind they know is far greater than their own.

We honor God with our trust. In return God honors us almost daily with fresh insight into what is true and good, and how to participate in it right now, where we find ourselves.

Day 169

God wants those around who are not naïve, who know full well there are "easier and faster" alternatives and yet still consciously choose to live in a state of voluntary dependence on a Greater Mind.

Only people who freely chose to trust God's ethical guidance, no matter what doing so costs them, can be trusted to take on delegated responsibility for the well-being of God's creation.

Day 170

There will be moments when it appears doing things God's ethical way will never work. Those who trust God are losing and those who don't are winning. Nevertheless, we still choose to hold tight to God's way, because we know in the depth of our hearts that God is good and does not mislead.

The ability to trust God freely, by choice, in the face of evidence that seems to contradict our learned confidence in God is a mental muscle we grow over time through exercise.

We can only practice voluntary dependence on a Greater Mind in real situations, not staged ones. And we must practice voluntary dependence behaviors enough times that they become reflexive.

Day 171

To obtain the coordinated action needed to build big things, the unnatural and godless civilizations that went before us used the threat of violence to force agreement, to secure resources, and to organize help.

Government is the only entity that can use the threat of violence or actual violence with impunity, so governments have always been the agents of the greatest, most destructive crimes against life.

Being forced under threat of violence to share resources is just another form of theft.

Being forced under threat of violence to provide help is just another form of slavery.

Being forced to agree under threat of violence is just another form of terror.

Day 172

Force causes loss. Loss causes resentment. Resentment never forgets, turns into hate, and waits for an opportunity to turn the tables. The cycle of violence continues ad nauseum, century after century - only the means of destruction become increasingly powerful.

God has nothing to do with anything that amounts to theft, slavery, or terror. So, we find other, peaceful ways to create consensus, share resources, and organize ourselves to do the tasks none of us can do alone.

This makes us distinctly different from the sickened majority. We don't cultivate resentment, so our solutions do not produce bigger problems between us or problems with our neighbors, waiting to erupt in the future.

Day 173

Con artists don't initially use the threat of violence. Rather, they cleverly manipulate and trick people into agreement, sharing resources, or providing help. Tricksters play on people's fears, desires, laziness, and vanity.

It is easy to spot a con artist; they are afraid of logical questions and don't want people to take time to think things through.

A con artist's solution always seems too good to be true. Something doesn't add up, something just feels off. You can't verify their claims. You're just supposed to trust them, and you are pressured to decide fast, so you won't miss out.

Day 174

Civilizations built on elaborate deceptions can only maintain themselves by producing ever larger, more elaborate deceptions, fables, and optical illusions, usually in the form of fantastic staged productions.

While we were still infected, we found ourselves first enthralled and enchanted, then later confused, and disappointed, living in the emptiness of the unfulfilled promise of the happy life captured in the carefully staged shows.

The prize always seemed a little farther off, but we never obtained it, or if we did, the prize did not live up to its billing and quickly soured.

Day 175

Diversity is about differences. Differences become painful when they lead to conflict. It is natural to want to relieve the pain as fast as possible.

In the middle of a difficult conflict between us there is a strong temptation to use force, or misleading promises to resolve the conflict quickly. However, we refuse to go down either of those roads.

If we use force now, in the future it produces resentment. Deception, once discovered, produces distrust in the future. Once people figure out an esteemed authority has tricked them the authority loses all authority. Now no one will believe the authority, even when it tells the truth. The benefit from lying is fleeting. The cost of lying endures for generations.

We learned from history that any mix of truth and lies, kindness and cunning, persuasion and threats turns out badly, no matter how successful it may be in the short term.

Day 176

God has called us to replace the old, dying, unjust civilizations we all came from with a new one that will naturally thrive as life on earth thrives, because it helps life in all its diversity thrive on the earth. God helps those who are helpful in this work, not those who won't.

We can't allow ourselves to repeat the mistakes of those who went before, no matter how indebted we may feel to them. Our ancestors were not the Creator and were fallible.

We commit ourselves to finding new solutions that require no force and require no fables, no fantasies to win hearts and minds.

Day 177

We are not afraid of reality, observation, facts, logical challenge, and the results of our experiments. We are not afraid to listen to our heart's longings, to feel and follow our loving trust and gratitude to God. We keep going.

The way out of conflict is through these difficulties. We make critical discoveries during the struggle. We learn nothing by ignoring or denying the need for struggle. Nothing improves by making excuses for harmful behaviors.

The still-infected want reality adjusted to them, as they are. Those who are becoming wise adjust to reality as it is. Reality is constantly changing, so constantly adjusting to our situation within God's ethical limits is the only approach that can secure a place for us on earth. Anything else leads to extinction.

Day 178

We find the path to our new sustainable civilization step by step; in the small solutions we work out together to address the daily difficulties and opportunities we face within our local reality.

Sometimes the way up to a new, higher solution is to go back to where those who went before us missed a turn. This means we must reject and undo something humans made earlier, something we inherited without question from others who lived before us.

We are not afraid of being wrong in our initial suggestions or solutions. We are not unduly afraid of abandoning an out-lived tradition. Our day is now, not then. Our situation is not what theirs was. God is our guide, not them.

Day 179

Sometimes we have a provisional method or tradition that got us through, but if we are honest we must admit it is not helpful anymore.

Just as a butterfly must tear open, exit, and abandon its chrysalis, we find if we follow the rules of life, at times we must break through and move beyond structures we or others worked hard on in the past. What was once solution is now a barrier to life's unfolding in our own time.

Our concern is not saving face or perpetuating an existing human institution. Our concern is restoring God's central place of honor in the affairs of humans.

God is honored only through the pursuit of what is true, what really works and promises to work in the future.

Day 180

We are not children and do not require fantastic fables, soothing promises, and easy answers. We don't look for magical solutions. We have learned that just because something makes us feel good quickly and easily does not mean it can create justice, turn out well, or be good for us.

The processes of nature are so ingenious and so astonishing we have no desire to claim solutions that appear nowhere in nature, as if God got it wrong.

Instead, we want to solve our problems in ways that more closely resemble the ways in which constant, emerging, changing complexity emerges in nature.

Clearly, that is the way God does things. And clearly, it produces wonderful results.

Day 181

God has made our lives into a complex, unfolding, changing, emerging entity that can serve as a uniquely creative part of the complex, unfolding, changing, emerging living whole that is the earth. The whole explains why our part exists and our part helps fulfill the purpose of the whole. There is no greater way to explain why we exist, no greater source of personal and collective meaning.

Under God's regenerating touch, we come to share the most striking quality *of* creation *with* creation - the ability to keep changing and growing in healthy ways that better fit us to our changing environment.

We adjust to the realities of life on life's terms.

We do not ask God to adjust reality to us so life can be easier. God's terms are there to uncover and learn, already embedded in the genius of life.

The more we work to understand life, the more we *can* adjust to it on its own terms, and the more satisfied we become with life.

Day 182

With the lifetime habit of adaptive growth as the theme of our stories, we show ourselves made of the same living tissue as the rest of life on earth. Earth no longer needs to reject us as something foreign, the way the body rejects foreign tissue.

We can be safely grafted into any wound, into any situation entrusted to us by God. Decay stops and regeneration commences.

An ethic that combines the habits of growth, transparent problem-solving, sustained dialogue, patience, and intellectual honesty makes us fit to do our God-given task anywhere on earth we are placed by fate.

Day 183

Our task is not to create something that will spread out rapidly in space, but something that will naturally extend itself slowly and securely far out in time, no matter what happens to it or around it.

Our species has an appointment to meet thousands of years in the future, and we must still exist and perform the complete function God intended for us to meet that appointment.

The unforeseen future of creation, known only to God, depends on how we choose to live today, right where we are, optimizing what God entrusted to us, with all its built-in differences and tension.

How we manage diversity now will determine if we still exist and are fit to fulfill our destined function then.

Day 184

At no time is being fitted to God's purposes more important than when we are working through a conflict, especially conflicts involving goals and values.

It is in conflict that we discover we are not yet fit to bring harmony out of conflict.

We call out to God and God starts a process that changes us so we can produce justice and productive peace between lives with different goals, needs, and values.

In our unfit condition our minds can't accurately update the mental model of ourselves to show our ethical deficits. We moved through the world thinking we were doing no harm, or that if we did, it didn't matter.

God teaches us the process of daily repentance. God updates our mental models daily, as we become aware of what we are currently incapable of doing.

Day 185

Because we love and trust God, the great healer, we accept and live with the pain of our incompleteness.

The pain keeps our attention directed where it needs to be directed. We respond to God's direction and correction until we begin to see different results when we interact with others. The pain starts to fade. Joyful freedom starts to take its place. We find we are now better fitted to the social situations God moves us into.

Our new fitness allows us to preserve and grow the diversity in which God so clearly delights. We become another quiet force of nature, in league with nature, following the laws of nature, participating in the unfolding of God's design.

Day 186

The laws of nature were not invented by humans and then mass marketed to make them popular and accepted. Rather, the laws of nature already exist. They are already there to be discovered by observation, then proven through successful experiments that others can replicate.

Since we are based in nature, we don't need or use propaganda. In nature, intimate, local, precisely timed and measured contact between two lives is how life finds its way into the future nature.

We broadcast nothing because there is no one solution for anything that matters that always fits all situations in all places. Knowing general notions about something is different from knowing it experientially and leads to serious mistakes.

Day 187

To follow the pattern of nature, to distribute vital information, we narrow-cast.

We hand on what we have learned about how God does happiness, change and diversity only to those who have deliberate prior first-hand learning already in place. God places in our place those who over time demonstrate competence and good intention.

Their own previous, costly efforts to understand what does and does not create justice prepare them to see the value in what we are sharing.

The prepared mind will see immediately how to use what we share to solve the problems in their own situation. The heart prepared by painful struggle and failure will be motivated to see a solution through until it works reliably to increase the stock of happiness in their own situation.

Day 188

We don't publicly assert that we have a better way of living together. That is far too easy to do and easy to falsify. The hard thing to do is to live together better when there is no audience to impress.

We simply prove we know a better way by living together constantly in a way that produces observable and measurable results which no other way of living together produces. Our results speak for themselves - we produce lives governed by the rules of life God put into all of creation.

Every life governed by God's rules of life becomes a community asset, providing services that increase the stock of happiness for everyone who shares a space with us.

Day 189

What proves the living presence of God in an individual is repentance – the ability to bear the pain of conscience that comes from harming another life through neglect or abuse, then harnessing that pain to replace harmful attitudes and behaviors with helpful ones.

Those who are not regenerating through direct contact with God, informed by nature cannot bear the pain of repentance.

If there is no remorse, there will be no change of heart. If there is no change of heart, there will be no real change in attitudes and behavior. If there is no real change in attitudes and behavior, there can be no change in what consumers and voters demand.

If there is no change in demand, there will be no change in what a civilization does to the earth.

Day 190

What proves the living presence of God among a group of people, is the ability to bear the pain that comes with struggling to resolve their differences without harming the God-given diversity among them. It is something those who are not regenerating simply cannot put group effort into.

If there is no creative struggle to deal with diversity, there will be no higher complexity. If there is no higher complexity, there will be no greater ability to cooperate. If there is no increase in the ability to cooperate, humanity will lack the very ability needed to respond to changes in the environment, especially sudden, big ones.

If there is insufficient ability to respond to big changes in the environment, there will be no future for humanity on earth.

Day 191

We have learned that if we give up our cooperative ethic to win an argument or power struggle, we forfeit something priceless and eternal to gain something cheap and fleeting.

We keep cooperating when cooperation is the hardest to do, not just when it is easy and fun.

Day 192

Adversity is what sometimes happens to us. Prosperity also sometimes happens to us. Prosperity does not change people; it allows them to be who they always wanted to be.

Adversity and prosperity reveal our Ethic.

Our Ethic is how we always, inevitably end up responding to what happens to us, especially as it affects the lives around us.

Our Ethic determines what we do and don't throw away under the pressure of possible loss or possible gain.

An ethic of cooperative helpfulness in adversity and prosperity defines a people in ways no marketing campaign can.

Day 193

Nature does not always reward selfishness with survival. With long-lived social species, nature rewards cooperation between members of the same species and between distinct species.

Natural cooperation happens first between those who share the same genes.

Healthy parents naturally want to see their children survive and thrive.

Healthy children naturally want their parents, grandparents, and siblings to live healthy, happy lives and to be part of their lives and their children's lives.

This natural first pathway to cooperation can break down, but it is unnatural and traumatic when it does.

Day 194

The next natural path to cooperation is what happens between those who are participating in direct reciprocity, each giving and receiving a benefit the other finds reliably helpful.

We naturally give the benefit of the doubt to those with whom we have a history of direct reciprocity when something goes wrong. We aren't eager to lose the benefit of the relationship. Most often we find it was just an unintended mistake or an honest misunderstanding. We quickly forgive and forget, as we would want them to do with us when we make a mistake or misspeak.

Those who forgive when it is warranted live longer and healthier than those who don't.

Day 195

The next natural pathway of cooperation is indirect reciprocity, which is what happens when someone's good reputation makes us inclined to trust them and try to work together.

A person or group's reputation comes from their ethic, whatever it may be.

Reputation precedes every individual and group and tells others what to expect should they cross their path. Reputation is the distillation of an individual or group's ethical system.

Just as a windsock doesn't lie, reputation also doesn't lie. It is an accurate predictor of future behavior because it accurately reflects the ethic of an individual or group.

Day 196

Since we don't abandon our ethic of cooperative helpfulness, especially when we are resolving conflict between us, our reputation sets the stage for those who have not yet met us to give us the benefit of the doubt.

If someone meets us and finds that our behavior matches our good reputation, that experience provides support to our account of what it is like to interact with directly with God. Our ongoing relationship with God is a satisfying explanation for why our kindness is authentic and dependable.

Find us to be genuine entices anyone placed in our path to seek God themselves, directly, informed by nature, because clearly something is happening to us and among us that is both uncommon and valuable.

In their own evitable moment of pain and confusion others are now more likely to cry out to their Creator, open to learning a new way to live.

Had we been mean to each other when we were in conflict we would have obstructed this third pathway to natural cooperation by creating own bad reputation.

Day 197

What is common among humans is to abandon their higher values when their interests are at stake. They assume God will not take care of them in a pinch, so they must do whatever it takes to take care of themselves, no matter who or what they harm.

What we do is uncommon. When we respond from the depths of our regenerating soul, from who we really are, we find we are always met, taught, and helped by God in ways we never could have planned.

We cooperate because now, as we live in a state of regeneration, we finally know this is who we humans really are - at the genetic level.

God made us to be helpful cooperators and to cultivate constructive cooperation anywhere we are placed on the earth, at any time, under any conditions.

Day 198

As God's change agents on earth, the way we work together during the most difficult times makes us demonstrably different. Over time we become so different, our values are so alien that we might as well be the beginning of a new species.

And who knows, perhaps we are. It is not our place to say. Only God knows.

In nature, one of the key functions of diversity is to lay the basis for new species that can survive in an environment the previous species could not. In our case, only time will tell.

Day 199

The ability to grow our empathy to match and govern our technical capacities is the essence of becoming wise. Wisdom is the skill of living life on life's terms.

Foolishness is trying to impose our terms on life, eventually damaging, and killing what we ourselves need to survive.

As long as our instinct for justice is too weak to limit our technical abilities we are not wise enough to prevent our own extinction and the extinction of many other species.

Any teaching that does not directly and constantly strengthen our instinct for justice, which does not embody an ethic of cooperative helpfulness is not wise, and is not from God.

God is the only One who is wise because true, complete, wisdom involves knowing everything without error. There is no truly wise human being, group, or nation.

Those who are being regenerated by choosing to maintain daily direct contact with God are those who never stop becoming wise. That's the best finite humans can do, but it is enough.

Day 200

Life is a system of interdependencies. Living systems and the relationships we create between each other that follow the rules that sustain living systems – these are the only things that can support our existence now and into a changing future.

Taking care of what takes care of us is central to understanding wise behavior.

Wisdom is not a set of concepts. Wisdom is a set of behaviors energized by a set of emotions – admiration, love, loyalty, trust, gratitude, contentment. '

Day 201

Any teaching that favors abstractions over behaviors is not natural.

Any teaching that discounts emotion or limits useful emotions to fear and greed is not from God.

The intellect is proud, cold, and hard. The intellect is the most common entry point for foolishness to enter our lives and the lives of our group.

The heart is humble, warm, and tender. Receptivity to divine wisdom comes only through humility and tender trust. Socially useful creativity is a function of empathy and intimacy.

Day 202

Creative intimacy is a function of direct, tender, gentle contact. Emotion alone can guide us to such contact and keep us there. Emotion is the most common entry point for wisdom to enter our lives and the lives of our group, starting with painful emotions.

God designed us to manage diversity. Managing diversity is our function on earth.

To manage diversity, we must live in a state of managed vulnerability that allows us to creatively engage ambiguity and constant change in such a way that builds an ever wider, more inclusive justice.

To manage vulnerability, we need a constant influx of current, relevant, divine wisdom.

If we close our hearts to emotional pain we also close our hearts to wisdom and to the joy that comes from feeling God's delight. God delights in nothing more than justice.

Day 203

To ignore, neglect, exploit or destroy what supports our own existence in the future just so we can enjoy some passing pleasure today is the essence of foolishness.

It is foolish to reject the pain that comes with adjusting to reality and demand that reality adjust to us so that we only experience pleasure.

We are foolish when we deliberately do things that we already know from history never end well in the attempt to create a life of all pleasure with no pain.

Day 204

Foolishness infuses itself with false ideas but is not itself a set of false ideas.

Foolishness is a set of *behaviors* energized by a set of *emotions* – fear, greed, envy, ingratitude, selfishness, arrogance, resentment.

While still infected we too lived in this foolish way because we too believed the purpose of life was to eliminate pain and pile up pleasures, no matter what the cost to the diversity of lives around us.

Now, every day, our behaviors move us a little bit farther away from foolishness and a little bit closer to wisdom.

God's happiness catches up to us on the path to wisdom, as we participate with increasing frequency in the beauty, creativity and diversity designed into life.

Day 205

We are forbearing with those who still live foolishly because we know we once were no different, if not worse.

Were it not for God' gracious and forceful intervention in our lives we too would still be getting ever more foolish, ever more harmful. Some of us felt God's intervention in the form of painful sadness and hopelessness. This pain is a natural alarm system God put in us to tell us we are on a path to extinction, to make us stop, cry out to God, and listen.

Some of us shut off the alarm and kept going. We felt God's firm opposition, even anger. It was just enough, just forceful enough, and lasted just long enough to stop us in our tracks and set us on a different path.

Day 206

Just as God stopped and redirected us, sometimes we must stop foolishness from taking root among us. We know it could harm the ethic of cooperative helpfulness we have worked so hard to build and put us back on the path to extinction.

Our first response is a sad silence that indicates we will not cooperate with what we are seeing.

If that does not work, we are prepared to actively oppose foolish attitudes and behaviors and let enough anger show to signal how seriously we take the reappearance of foolish selfishness among us.

Day 207

Just as our hands cannot grip something without an opposing thumb, we can't take hold of a situation that is getting worse without opposing selfish behavior as soon as it shows up.

The evidence of an increase in wisdom is the ability to use anger properly, just as God did with us when we were harming others.

There is nothing wrong with anger. God gave us anger as a defense when what God provided to sustain our lives comes under threat.

There *is* something wrong with the foolish *mismanagement* of anger.

Day 208

To paraphrase Aristotle, once we can be angry at the right time, in the right way, for the right amount of time, toward the right person, for the right reason, we have clearly become wiser than we used to be.

Only when we effectively control our anger can we extend the authority of God into a chaotic situation. When we do this effectively, bad things can stop happening and something new and better can start happening. These interventions are as rare as they are crucial.

We don't go looking for them, but neither do we run away when a skilled intervention is necessary to prevent more harm.

Day 209

A society is composed of individuals who make their lives within it.

The average quality of its individuals forms a hard limit on how sane and just <u>any society can be. Yet the existing society is what rewards or withholds rewards from individuals, so the average person becomes no better than what society will reward.</u>

In a kind of vicious circle, an unjust society produces unjust individuals whose expectations and demands limit tell its leaders what to promise. Leaders chase the crowd's approval and then "lead the people" in circles, going nowhere but farther down the drain into chaos.

Only God can reverse this cycle and starts the only place the new can be born, in the heart of an individual.

Day 210

A selfish society will discourage cooperative helpfulness by reserving its richest rewards for its most selfish members, making its most ethical people look like naïve fools.

The rare, ethical individual will find it far more difficult than the selfish person to attract a mate or prosper in their work, reducing their numbers even further, making their kind even rarer.

Yet a new, sustainable civilization can only be built after the emergence of a new kind of individual human, one in which self-regulation is normal, strong and grows stronger over their lifetime.

Day 211

We are the lonely few whose individual, daily choices, guided by God and informed by nature, are new, different, and better than what the society around us will ever understand, acknowledge, or reward.

As in nature, God quietly deploys the rarest and most unusual members of a species to found new colonies of life. We set to work out on the margins, out of sight, away from the chaos and collapse the old species has brought on itself through its selfishness.

Our first task is to make the most of the diversity of life God has already entrusted us with.

Day 212

Anyone from any background can be part of what we are working toward as long as they want nothing more passionately than to participate in God's completion of the human project on God's terms for God's purposes.

In fact, only God's power can restore any individual human from any and every background. None of us have the knowledge to know what someone from a completely different background must go through to fully heal and start regenerating because their story is not our story.

God alone is the ultimate physician and builder.

Day 213

In history, revolutionaries and reformers have often been more hateful to each other than to the systems they tried to reform and replace. Each camp believed those with a rival approach stood in the way of the ultimate good, so any action needed to remove them was justified. Their own internal rivalries proved they had nothing in hand that was qualitatively better than what they were trying to fix.

Successfully including others from all backgrounds, from any point of view, is the only proof that God is at work among us. If we can't do that, we are no different than all the failed attempts to reform humanity that have gone before.

Day 214

The challenge of bringing unity out of diversity is the acid test for any endeavor that claims to be a work of God or claims it can bring a better future.

The successful management of diversity is the only reliable leading indicator that something good is already happening and something even better is coming.

Day 215

God's goodness catches up with those who seek justice at every level of their lives. It starts with giving God what God alone is due. Anything less is unjust.

We stop giving any human, any human organization, or any other created thing the attention, admiration, trust, and receptivity that only The Creator deserves.

Only then does God's goodness start to inform and change the relationship we have with our own self. Only then do painful internal conflicts start to resolve.

Day 216

Once we finally understand that we are not the center of the universe..

Once we know in our bones that we don't and can't know what is best to want...

Once we see that it is offensive to try to use God's power to get what we want...

Once we grasp that we exist to help further God's purposes on earth...

Once we accept that our God-given life is not about piling up pleasures and avoiding pain at all costs...

THEN God starts to meet us daily, in solitude, deep inside our souls with a steady, guiding, healing touch.

Day 217

We experience God's presence on God's terms or not at all.

God helps those who intend to be helpful and locks out those who don't.

Being locked out of God's presence means living with the absence of the divine, which creates a painful emptiness. Emptiness sucks in all sorts of filth, lies, half-truths, delusions, and destructive habits, and makes us easy prey for clever predators and parasites.

Once we truly decide to be helpful, God helps us reconcile all the different and quarreling parts of our own souls. The emptiness starts to be filled with a growing peace.

Day 218

Once we start to live in a more internally unified state, God's goodness can and does flow out of our solitude and into our relationship with other lives, whether human or not. We find it is natural and pleasing to be careful with anything God created.

Our own personal experience with becoming more unified internally helps us accept that it will take time, attention, and struggle to achieve external unity, while making sure each fellow creature retains what is theirs by divine right.

We start to actively help God do diversity. God starts things. God creates. We help what God creates flourish. We fulfill the reason humanity exists and feel fulfillment in ways we never knew were possible. Rather than feeling empty, we feel full to overflowing.

Day 219

Bringing justice to diversity is not a quick or easy process. There is no gimmick. No one else can do it for us.

There are moments when a lot happens fast, but most of the time things happen slowly. But things do happen under God's direction that never happen otherwise.

All the most precious things in life come into being through sustained personal and group investments of time and attention. A just and rich diversity is no different.

Day 220

Justice with diversity is the seal of divine authenticity. It produces natural complexity – the combination of high differentiation and high organization.

Natural complexity is an energized stability, a system that never stops changing yet retains the signature of divine design – high diversity and high cooperation.

It is stable enough for new forms of life to get started, but not so stable it can't change when conditions change.

In God's natural justice there is neither violent chaos nor stagnant rigidity, so we refuse to participate in either of those extremes.

Day 221

A just and rich diversity often uses space to solve problems.

Individuals of the same species spread out enough but not too much. Different species in the same area also spread out but not too much.

Get too far apart and we lose the benefit of being together, get too close together and a population can cause problems for itself that are bigger than anything in the environment.

With higher population density there are more collisions. Epidemics are more frequent, intense, and longer lasting. Demand for resources outstrips the resources that lie nearby. Water and air become more polluted.

Day 222

We give people time and space to think and reach their own conclusions for their own reasons. We accept the challenge God has given humanity to help cultivate the fulness of creation, right where we are in the situation we face.

We don't wait for perfect conditions. We continue to engage each other until we see our differences come together to form a higher, more complex, sturdier well-being.

A sturdy, energized, widely shared well-being is the only thing that can carry our kind far into the future so we can be there to take care of all other kinds of life God will entrust to our care.

Day 223

The best thing we can do to manage diversity is to allow each different type of life to have and manage its own space.

We confront another life's behavior only if it materially injures our own body, takes away the local resources God distributed to us to sustain our own body and the bodies of our family. We also confront behavior that harms the relationship between us, making it impossible to continue to share a space.

Otherwise, we leave others alone without comment.

We may not approve of what they do but we do not impose our way of doing things on them. We also don't let them impose their way of doing things on us.

Just because we imagine some future harm that might come from how they behave does not mean we are authorized to meddle in the way they choose to live.

Day 224

Study any thriving ecosystem and you will see creatures that behave differently from each other living right alongside each other, largely without conflict.

In contrast, among humans at least 70% of the unproductive tension and conflict that arises from differences is the result of one individual or group imposing its own behaviors on another without permission.

It is best to share another way of doing things if sought out and asked. Second best is to sometimes offer another option gently, quietly, in private, starting with a non-threatening question – "There is another approach with a good track record. Would you like to discuss it?"

Day 225

It would be as unnatural for us to go out and seek to convert anyone as it would be for a tree to try to change a bird into a tree, so it can have a bigger grove.

If a tree does what a tree does well, the bird may discover life is better around the tree than away from the tree. In time, the two work out a way to help each other along. The result is more and healthy birds, and in time, a larger grove of trees as the bird, which is mobile, helps the tree, which is stationary – to distribute its seeds after eating its fruit.

Day 226

All life naturally seeks connection and combination. At the same time, the drive for space in creatures is as strong as the drive for food. Nature balances attraction toward each other and repulsion away from each other leading to a distributed pattern of habitats and their inhabitants.

We like being around each other and avoid being completely isolated. Creatures from distinct species that peacefully share a space can warn each other of danger, simply by warning their own kind of danger.

Creatures that survive by staying near enough to each other live longer and can raise offspring that live long enough to do the same.

Day 227

We let nature take its surprising course. We live our way and let others live their way. We do not interfere with them in their space, and we don't let them interfere with us in ours.

We do look for ways to benefit them at little or no cost to us. We find that often, they start to do the same, because the exchange is enjoyable and useful.

Day 228

When the outcome of a behavior is better than we had before and the experience of creating it was enjoyable, we naturally want to repeat the behavior.

This natural desire to make contact again indicates a bond is forming between us and another of God's creatures.

Day 229

A bond has formed when we realize that we would miss their presence if they were not around. By being different from us, somehow they lighten our burden and increase our happiness, as we do for them.

The experience of reliable mutual benefit starts to cure the pain of loneliness. We start to feel less of the anxiety and dread that comes from feeling that no one would be there to help in a crisis.

Day 230

Natural bonds break when one person alone pays the cost of cooperation and the other gets the benefit, while paying no cost. No relationship can survive if this continues.

God's justice distributes costs and benefits to everyone in a group equally, with each bearing a cost that is equal to their abilities, while constantly growing those abilities.

In God's justice, with each growth in ability and resources there comes an increase in responsibility. In a godly society we are always accountable to each other, and responsible for each other when one of us cannot meet his or her own needs.

In nature, God does not permanently burden some members of a species to benefit others who permanently bear no burden.

Day 231

In God's justice, burden shifting happens, but only while a member of a social species cannot bear the full burden of its own existence, such as in infancy, old age, sickness, injury, or disability.

No one wants to feel like a burden to others and God wants no one to feel that way. Everyone has some deficit whether or not it is currently visible. Everyone has some surplus, whether or not it is currently visible. It is possible to be very useful to God's purposes even while one's usefulness to others is not yet apparent.

Day 232

Among us each member of the group bears as much of the weight of its own existence as it can and helps the group bear burdens no individual can bear alone, as much as it can. This combination of as much self-sufficiency as possible with as much contribution to the group's needs as possible gives every member standing, dignity and a sense of belonging.

In nature, among social species, those who can bear the burden of their own existence to some degree but don't, who can contribute to the group's efforts, but don't - are confronted and driven off, not rewarded.

Day 233

We are called to found and fund a new civilization through the investment of our God-given time, energy, attention, and talent.

Previous civilizations were founded mostly on what people at the top were able to *get* for themselves by organizing everyone else the way they did.

We do our founding work mostly by what we willingly cultivate and give, not by what we greedily demand and scheme to get.

Our new discoveries are labors of love. This work will require the best we have for the rest of our lives.

Day 234

We don't haggle with God to arrive at a minimum amount we must give back to God and earth. We don't think it is all about us, nor do we feel that God's expectations are a nuisance. We don't think the protection of life on earth is a burden. Rather, we think it is a privilege to undertake.

We don't think once we have given 10% of our income to God we can' use the rest any way we want. We don't think once we have set aside one day a week for God, we can use the rest of the week to do anything we want, any way we want.

Those negotiated minimums can build buildings and pay salaries, but they have never been enough to create widespread justice. God is not cheap and stingy toward us. We are not cheap and stingy toward God.

Day 235

God gave us life as a part of earth. Earth is extremely rare, perhaps unique in the universe it is ability to support complex life. Earth gave us everything we have and made us everything we are.

In return we owe God and earth everything we have and everything we are. As we repay our debts to God and earth with gifts of careful justice, both God and earth respond by enveloping us in their purposes.

We give of ourselves. We give the best we have been given. We hold back no time, effort, attention, or struggle, be it emotional, social, or technical if it is necessary to do what is just.

Day 236

Genetically, no matter what our background, all current humans are the same. Differences in skin color, facial features and hair are not enough to make us functionally different from each other.

Yet we are all significantly different from our nearest primate relatives.

What separates humans from other primates is entirely regulatory, a combination of epigenetic mechanisms that turn on and off traits that all other primates also have.

Self-regulation from the inside out is the very essence of being truly human. Any loss in our ability to self-regulate is a loss of our essential humanity.

Day 237

We find it is possible to self-regulate just as long and just as well as we each individually remain in constant, direct contact with God - our ultimate environment, and with nature, our immediate environment.

Making contact with a human representative of God or an artistic representation of God - is not making contact with God. Making contact with a substitute, something that claims to be better than God - is not making contact with God.

Making contact with any artificial, built environment is not making contact with nature. Making contact with artistic or photographic representations of nature is not making contact with nature.

At best, any representation can only direct us to go see for ourselves. It cannot take the place of living contact with life in all its diversity, intelligence, and power.

Day 238

Any form of false contact with God serves only to sever contact with God.

Any form of false contact with nature serves only to sever contact with nature.

Severed contact causes the loss of self-regulation, which is necessary to cooperate with each other enough to create justice out of diversity.

Day 239

Self-regulation is the only thing that makes us truly human, both individually and in groups. As along as our behavior is regulated from outside ourselves by any force other than God, our evolution into a constructive species stops. Our decay into an ever more destructive species accelerates.

The recovery of real direct contact with God and nature, in solitude, is the only thing that can begin to restore our ability to limit, regulate and re-direct our amazing productive capacities. Self-regulation is functional wisdom.

This distinction between real and false contact is so vital we are vigilant about the reintroduction of anything that replaces direct contact with God and nature.

Day 240

Vigilance is the test of full maturity and shows itself in readiness.

Vigilance is a state of low work but high attention, ready to spring into full work mode on a moment's notice.

Our body's immune system exists in a state of constant vigilance. It responds immediately when it detects a pathogen or foreign agent in the body.

So do we, when we detect the introduction of an idea or behavior that would redirect our attention and dependence away from the Creator and on to something created.

Day 241

To live in a way so new and unfamiliar to the still-sickened majority, we need new, reliable, role models, for whom this way of living is normal.

Role models prove a new way of living is possible and desirable. A good role model typically demonstrates that the cost of living differently is less than we thought, and the reward is more than we thought.

An older, wiser species with a better track record is a better role model than any human or human group.

(We didn't study each other to invent airplanes, we studied birds.)

Day 242

Because we need reliable role models, we naturally love trees and seek their company.

We make direct quiet contact with God among them.

We don't worship trees because like us, they are creatures, not the Creator. But we worship with them around us because unlike humans, trees have never severed contact with the flow of divine intelligence or with the rest of nature around them.

Our choice of models determines what we become. We become like whatever and whomever we focus on and admire. Trees make better role models than any imaginary person from the past or current celebrity because we can verify for ourselves what the nearby individual trees do and don't do, now and over the course of time.

With trees we don't have to rely on carefully crafted public personas in media reports or on ancient fables, neither of which we can verify. Trees have never lost their essentially social, cooperative nature.

Just as having a great natural athlete on a team makes everyone else on the team better, having a creature near us that lives the way we must relearn to live, sets our sights higher and makes us better.

Trees show us how it is done and prove it can be done.

Day 243

One of the most striking things about trees is that they maintain constant contact with the sun and the soil. If they lose contact with either, they die. If they maintain contact, they never stop growing.

Something about making and sustaining direct contact with what is larger and older than us activates our cooperative abilities and keeps them growing stronger.

Like the trees, we never go a day without using our regenerating social capacities, so we never have a day that we don't grow in our creative and ethical skills or at least outgrow something that was never very helpful in the first place.

Day 244

There is something about losing direct contact with God and nature or only trying to make contact on occasion in a crisis, which causes our cooperative abilities to stop growing and start to dry out, harden, and wither away.

Since our cooperative abilities use neuropathways, like all others, they are plastic. Something plastic takes on a new shape and does not return to the one it had before. When God awakens and sustains our dormant cooperative abilities they take on a new shape and strongly resist going back.

Conversely, when we stop using our cooperative abilities daily, they take on a stunted, frozen, useless form and strongly resist going back to their natural, healthy function.

Day 245

We are becoming wise to the extent that we can self-regulate. We are self-regulating if we are limiting our selfishness to hold open a space for a cooperative solution to emerge.

When we abandon or lose direct contact with God and nature, we become dangerous to ourselves and other lives as we give freer and freer rein to our selfishness.

In that foolish, dangerous state, adding speed and mass is not a solution, but a problem leading to extinction.

Day 246

To keep our cooperative abilities healthy and growing, we use goals in a new way. Goals help humans focus their energies, both individually and collectively, but they are creations, they are no substitute for The Creator's involvement in our endeavors.

Before entering the process of regeneration, while still infected by unlimited selfishness we loved our goals. If we believed in God at all, we tried to commandeer God's assistance to reach our goals faster, with less effort. In essence, we loved goals and tried to use God.

The history of religion is mostly a series of gimmicks to get God to help humans achieve their goals. The whole enterprise assumed humans knew best and could manipulate God.

It reflected the uncooperative, demanding attitude of a child, not the attitude of a mature and loving adult.

Day 247

Once we learn to make and sustain direct contact with God and nature, we feel how offensive it is to love anything more than God and to try to use our Creator like some kind of utensil to get what we want.

As long as we are regenerating we know we don't know what is best because we don't know the future. Yet goals are still useful for focusing our energies.

What makes us different now is that we love God permanently, and use adjustable goals temporarily, as far as they are useful to creating justice and cultivating diversity.

Day 248

When we love our goals more than God, if someone gets in the way of a goal we will suspend God's ethical limits and do whatever it takes to get that person out of our way, so we can achieve our goal.

When we love God more than any goal, when someone gets in the way of our goal, we stop and earnestly seek God, then wait for ethical guidance. Nothing is more important in a conflict than divine ethical direction. Divine direction will always further the well-being of the whole system of interacting lives, not just one participating life or group. How to do that is rarely obvious or easy.

Day 249

We refuse to suspend God's limits on how we treat each other as a way of "staying on schedule." Goals, plans, and schedules are helpful, but all those human creations combined add up to nothing compared to the astonishing, active help of God.

We never risk losing God's involvement in our work just so we can see our plans progress. God does not honor and protect plans. God honors and protects listening and responsive loyalty to divine priorities.

Day 250

We create relationships between ourselves by doing practical things that need to be done - with each other and for each other.

Conflict between us usually arises over sharing a limited resource or managing a task that requires one of us to depend upon the work of another before we can continue our work and do it well.

We must learn to share a limited resource ethically and efficiently. We must learn to hand our task off to the next person who is counting on us to do our part well and on time.

Day 251

If the way we hand off a task is unhelpful and makes the other person's task harder to do well and on time, we are acting in a way that is both unethical and inefficient.

Indifference to the experience we are creating for our teammate is evidence that we are not recovering from the sickness of unlimited selfishness.

If we hand off a task in such a way that the next person is more able to do their part well and on time, we are clearly recovering from the sickness of unlimited selfishness.

As founders of a new civilization, it is our duty to leave behind a religious, economic, and social system that is a pleasure to manage, not a disaster waiting to happen.

Day 252

The way we fulfill our duty to those who will come after us is to use these teamwork lessons to take on ever more complex and promising assignments from God. On each round our confidence in God, ourselves, each other, and our team grows, as it should.

Under God's direction and cultivation, we resolve the tensions that came from sharing limited resources and coordinating our efforts while staying within God's ethical limits. Since we don't lapse back into unlimited selfishness, our growing confidence in our team is well earned.

We have proven to ourselves we can do it, even when it is frightening and difficult. We have good reason to believe we can do it again and will do it again. By passing on orally the lessons we learned through first-hand struggle, we equip those who follow us to deal with the problems of diversity that will inevitably arise.

Day 253

There is another kind of conflict between us that is more challenging to resolve than sharing limited resources and coordinating efforts. It is a conflict in goals.

Two people or groups can be good at sharing resources and coordinating efforts and yet still have a relationship-threatening conflict when their goals diverge.

Day 254

When our goals diverge it makes all the difference in the world whether we love our goals more than we love God. If we spend time daily listening to God's quiet voice, we will love God more than anything. If we spend time daily listening to other voices, including our own, we will love other things more than God.

If we love our goals more than God, in a conflict we will abandon God's priorities and double our efforts to achieve our goal, even if that means harming someone who has done us no harm, but who simply disagrees about what the next goal we should work on together.

If we love God more than our goals, we know anything created can be modified or even abandoned, but we can't let go of our Creator.

Day 255

When we find ourselves holding tightly to divergent or opposing goals, neither of us expects the other to defer. Neither of us tries to force or trick the other into deferring. We listen to each other. We use verifiable facts. We reason together. We learn with and from each other until we understand our shared situation better.

Even still, sometimes we come to an impasse.

We both defer to God. We acknowledge that God alone knows what is best, what next action will help extend the rule of divine goodness on earth, not only in space, but in time.

Day 256

We don't have a crystal ball. No one does.

Unlike God...

We can't foresee the future.

We can't know the thoughts and true intentions of others.

We can't see in advance the unintended consequences of our actions.

We can't predict events in the world that could disrupt either of our goals.

We can't foresee an opening that creates better options than either of our divergent approaches could ever make possible.

Day 257

When we are still infected with unlimited selfishness we use a crystal ball. We look into the magic ball and foresee a terrible future filled with misery. We act to prevent that terrible future and end up setting in motion the very thing we fear.

When we are recovering from the sickness we throw away our crystal ball. We live in a state of receptive, responsive, adaptation.

We are directed daily and frequently corrected to stay within God' ethical limits. We don't say things that create unnecessary problems between us. We don't do things that make others resentful and less willing to cooperate to solve problems.

Day 258

When we are in a conflict situation, we remain aware that we are in a perilous situation. Even though we have thrown out our crystal ball we still know things could go wrong.

We must be careful - full of care.

Behaving with slow, tender carefulness is a natural response to seeing an infant who is helpless and totally dependent on us to survive. God gave us this response as a way to protect life when life cannot protect itself.

Tender carefulness is also the natural, healthy response to a conflict between us that arises from our diversity.

Day 259

In a conflict we work to remain even more aware of God's presence and wisdom to guide us - word by word, step by step, decision by decision.

We stay in this state of tender carefulness all the way through the perilous situation until we enter a new one with better possibilities than were there before.

The perilous passage itself draws out new capacities in us individually and collectively that we will use to create a new, broader, sturdier justice between us, with all our God-given differences still intact.

We emerge as a better team. Often we emerge as a team of teams.

Day 260

What does tender carefulness look like when we engage in a conflict?

Alone with our Creator, informed by the genius embedded in nature each of us cries out...

"Dear God, please help me. Help me see, feel, hear, know, become, embody, and enact what your justice requires now in this situation.

Yesterday's solutions can't solve today's problems. I know I don't know what is best and I know you do.

I fear the consequences if we can't resolve this conflict in a way that honors you and teaches both of us more about the way you do things."

Then we fall silent, wait, watch, and listen. We have created an open, holy place where we are most likely to be met, touched, taught, and helped by God. We are about to witness first-hand how God does diversity. It will be a solution we never could have anticipated, but once seen, we realize it could not possibly be better.

Day 261

We stay as *fluid* in our responses to the situation we face as we stay *fixed* in our dependence upon God. We fasten tightly to God and fit and refit our choices to the needs we observe.

We stand ready to alter anything in our assumptions, attitudes, choices, and behaviors which God show us must change. We limit our certainty and selfishness to create an open space, an indefinite, ambiguous, flowing space where we will be met by our Creator, and meet each other's needs in ways we have not yet done before.

Initially there is only an abyss, an impasse. We see nothing. We fear nothingness will envelop us and our endeavors. Yet we know that God alone creates something out of nothing. God alone brings out of chaos a new and higher, more complex, more resilient order.

Day 262

In an impasse between us what we seek and hold out for is the unforeseen, creative opening only God can create.

We know that neither of us who are party to a conflict, nor our relationship, nor our situation will ever be the same after God meets us in an opening in which God meets us, teaches us, and helps us.

We experience moments of creation as fully invested participants, not as detached, theoretical observers. We learn that these moments of creation are precisely what God made humans for.

Day 263

As we are regenerating it is not obvious error that causes the most frightening conflicts between us, as if one of us is all right and one of us is all wrong. Rather, what causes severe conflicts is that both of us hold some mix of truth and error. Our personal mix of truth and error is something we silently ask others to overlook and include in whatever solution we produce.

Since it is possible to mislead someone else it is not only possible, but likely that we have been misled, sometimes by very sincere and caring people, who may have been misled themselves.

Day 264

When we are in a conflict around competing goals, we typically cannot see where we have been misled. We all have blind spots. We can be blind to our own unverified assumptions, our own mix of truths, half-truths, and errors. We can also be simply naïve because we lack direct personal experience with the issue with which we are wrestling.

We also often don't see any unhelpful attitude we may have because we are blinded by our own certainty that we know best.

Equal and opposite untested certainties can converge to create an impasse. It is often in just such an impasse that we find a divinely given opportunity for profound change in ourselves, our relationship and in our shared situation.

Day 265

The one who disagrees with us is the one who can see where we have been misled with razor sharp precision, just as we can see where they have been misled with perfect clarity.

In God's mercy, we are provided strong and capable teammates who can reveal our own mix of truth and error. They use facts and logic in a way that stops us in our tracks.

In this way God prevents us from doing harm to ourselves and others in a future we cannot foresee, often simply because in our certainty we would have been blinded to a possibility that is better than anything humans have done in the past. Certainty comes at the expense of astonished wonder.

We are a people who live in a state of astonished wonder much of the time. It is what one feels in the presence of the infinitely creative mind that is God.

Day 266

The civilization God is founding is built out of what we willingly give to the effort. Yet crucially, it is protected and secured in advance by what we willingly give up because something better is now possible, given new information we did not have before.

We all bring with us cherished notions, often ancient in origin, which we're taught come from God. We overlook the fact that the entire history of that notion, when put into action, when institutionalized, is littered with injustice and harm to innocent lives.

Day 267

When God puts someone we love and need in our path who passionately disagrees with us, we must make a choice. Will we be loyal to our Creator, who wants us to cooperate with living, real people divinely placed in our lives right now?

Or will we be loyal to some distant idealized person or cherished notion from the past?

If we are loyal to anything other than our Creator, we can easily become uncooperative with the real living people who have been placed in our lives.

Day 268

Through the process of ethically resolving conflicts involving goals and values, both parties to a conflict of goals can identify and discard their our own untested falsehoods while embracing even more tightly our newly verified certainties - insights into how God works that are true for all life everywhere for all time.

Our shared, newly purified understanding of the reality we confront forms a solid foundation upon which to start over, creating a society that honors God's priorities and takes care of God's Creation as its first and central purpose, not as an afterthought.

Day 269

The falsehood or half-truth we are clinging to in a conflict is often the cherished remnant of an old solution to one of the enduring problems that come with being human and sharing the earth with other creatures. It was perhaps the best our ancestors could do or chose to do at the time.

However, no matter how valuable their contribution, they were still created beings, not the uncreated Creator.

To be fair, our ancestors had less information about how nature solves problems than we do now. In the absence of good information about how nature solves a certain class of problems, our ancestors used imaginative guesswork.

Guesswork is a kind of putty used to fill the gaps in what we know. Putty masks problems but inevitably dries out, cracks, and falls off, revealing problems that have gotten worse for lack of accurately informed action.

Day 270

God, the author of life, has better, higher, completely unforeseen solutions to the still unsolved problems a human society must solve together. In a conflict, we often realize we are working on a small, local version of a larger problem that touches more than just us.

God is using our intimate local conflict to guide all of us out of the old, failed solutions and into new and better ones. We are trail blazers, going where no foot has trod before, headed to a place people have not inhabited in a long time, if ever.

But first we pass through a place devoid of the old solutions all of us brought with us but also lacking a better new solution to take the place of our old, now discredited certainties.

Day 271

An unresolved conflict is a moment of crisis.

The guesswork putty from the past is cracking and falling off, but right now there is nothing true and available to take its place. We need something that embodies the genius of life's natural problem-solving ability.

In the gap between the old and familiar that doesn't create justice, and the new and unfamiliar that will one day create justice, we are left in limbo lacking both stability and certainty.

Day 272

Humans naturally fear instability and ambiguity. Until we have been personally met in such an empty and dark place, we don't yet know first-hand the sufficiency of God's grace, the power of God's touch, and the superiority of God's wisdom.

Ambiguity and instability are frightening. Our fear serves us well if it causes us to slow down, open our minds to new information about how nature solves the kind of problem we are facing, and pay very close attention to what we learn, and be ready to act on it.

However, in our fear we are tempted to settle for less than God's best. If we do, less is what we will get and pass on to those who follow us. We will have passed on a festering problem, not a new solution.

Day 273

If instead of succumbing to fear, trusting only what the impatient eye can see, we choose to trust God's omniscience as we see proven in nature. For a time, we will have no idea what form God's creative solution will take. We wait, watch and listen.

If we use the patient eye and hold out for God's best, God's best is what we get and what we will pass on to those who come after us.

We will have passed on a solution that will allow our descendants to address the next set of unsolved problems in a much stronger position. In this way, life moves on, and we move on within life with God.

Day 274

The unnerving gap in certainty is a holy place, the only place where the useful new is born.

This indefinite, mysterious place holds answers to questions we don't yet know how to ask. It pulses with the most and best creative options.

Without realizing it, without intending to, we have crossed the threshold into the sublime. We are now assistants to the Creator, working in the inner chamber, working on the creation of new life.

And it never would have happened without the conflict that arose from our differences, from our diversity.

Day 275

Without our differences and the conflicts that arise from them, useful new solutions will never come into the world.

The truly new is neither a modified version, nor an improvement, or extension of what we have always done. The conflict itself is evidence that the truly new does not yet exist and it is our job to create it carefully, under God's supervision,.

The truly new is a leap, a discontinuity, a break from what we have always done as humans. It is a welcome departure that promises outcomes humans have never been able to achieve when motivated by fear and greed, trusting in their own finite intelligence.

Day 276

The truly new is not a novel, clever move within a known set of rules, trying to win a tired old game - because creation is not game playing. True creation is a function of intimate, trusting contact, not ambitious competition.

The truly new comes from accepting a completely new set of rules, the rules of profound and lasting creativity.

When we shift up to this higher set of rules we find ourselves able to adjust our actions to our changing situation in ways we never could have before.

Day 277

It takes courage to leap up into a new, higher set of rules. But it is not a leap into the dark, but up into greater sanity and a deeper understanding of how life itself solves problems.

Courage is not a leap of faith in the sense of trying to believe nonsensical fables about events unlike anything we have ever seen first-hand, that supposedly happened to people we have never met.

Rather, our leap of faith is a leap to catch up with what other creatures, older and wiser than us have been doing to solve their problems for millions of years. Physically when we leap, we leave something behind and quickly arrive at a new place. Courage is no different.

To make occasional, necessary, natural, rational, fact-and-logic based leaps, we will need to become conversant with real functional courage.

Day 278

Courage comes from the personal experience of being deeply loved. After taking part in the process of regeneration for some time we know we are deeply loved and valued. Through it all we were never coddled but never abandoned either. We suffered pain and loss, but our ability to be useful to God and helpful to life was never irreparably harmed. Instead, we became more available and more useful to God.

Those who have never known loss will come to love things that promise to prevent loss; these are usually wasteful human creations.

We who have recovered from loss come to love what restores, renews and replaces with something functionally better after loss. Only life itself can do that. And life is a creation of God alone.

Day 279

After recovering from loss and setbacks we are connected to the One who restores, renews, and replaces what was lost with something more valuable. As a result, we know if it is again necessary to take a risk that could cause loss, we can keep moving forward in the face of risk.

Courage is not the absence of fear in the face of necessary risk.

Courage emerges naturally as a side effect of knowing from experience those experiences we don't need to fear any more than necessary. We need enough fear to prepare and adapt to the situation we are entering, but no more. And no less.

Day 280

Sometimes, to achieve a just diversity it is necessary to enter into conflict. Sometimes the conflict is not between right and wrong, but between two things that are both right, or at least have strong, logical arguments behind them based in verifiable facts.

We have learned from experience not to fear that God will abandon us in a necessary conflict, so we don't freeze, flee or attack each other.

Instead, we look to God, the only One who knows the way through.

In spite of our fear, we keep moving daily, up toward God's best and away from solutions that cratered at the very moments humans most needed to work together in the past.

Day 281

As two hikers both approach the same summit, but from opposite sides of the mountain, the distance between them diminishes. They are not pursuing closeness to each other, they are pursuing the highest, the crest, the place with the longest and best view.

Resolving a conflict that comes from our God-given diversity is like hiking up a steep mountain face. It is hard work, but different from how we moved before we began our ascent. When walking or running on flat ground or a slight incline we take many strides quickly, but none of them require intense effort, and none of them make a significant difference in our elevation. We move farther in distance but little in height.

In contrast, once we begin to ascend to the crest we take fewer steps, we move more slowly, and each step requires more intense effort, but each one moves us higher, to a significant degree. Our gain in elevation is measurable and observable, along with our temporary fatigue.

When God is directing the work, we find ourselves tired *in* the work, but it just too interesting to become tired *of* the work.

Day 282

When climbing a mountain, what we lose in speed, distance covered, and ease, we gain in elevation and perspective.

Facing a conflict involving a valued team member is like climbing a mountain, starting from opposite sides. At high elevation open to a vast expanse, both parties can take in things instantly that might have escaped you both altogether. After the long struggle, at the shared peak you see patterns in the landscape that can only be observed very slowly had you continued to move along quickly on easy ground.

Not all difficulty yields higher complexity, but facing a necessary, God-given difficulty always has that potential. For members of a social species engaged in an important shared endeavor, being opposed by a valued teammate with a good factual argument is one of those divine difficulties.

These necessary and natural conflicts are pregnant with creative possibilities in a way few other encounters in life are.

Day 283

As a natural side effect of pursuing the same ultimate goal, a strange togetherness ensues between us, even if we are approaching the problem from opposite points of view.

We both become intimately familiar with the terrain and the real challenges in solving our shared problem. We have more in common with each other than with all of those who are not trying to climb the mountain.

Day 284

Just as in climbing a mountain, if we both share the same ultimate goal – to create a solution that reflects the healing wisdom of God, we shed once cherished proximate goals that are no longer useful to advance our ultimate goal.

Mountain climbers carry no unnecessary baggage with them. In a similar way, we all shed old, outlived guesswork and replace it with hard-won facts, as we learn more from nature than from human culture.

We approach the crest. To our thrilled astonishment we enter a new, higher, stronger harmony. We make productive use of our differences in ways that complete each other, while trimming away old errors we inherited from well-meaning, but fallible, humans.

As old, dried out errors fall away, healthy, new organic growth begins to take its place. We get to witness God's regenerative process and power, the very essence of life itself.

Day 285

Mountains can teach the larger, older lessons of life, when we engage them directly using personal effort, while carefully managing the real risks that come with doing so.

So do forests.

And rivers and river valleys.

Along with grasslands and wetlands.

So do deserts and tidepools, and the oceans from which we all evolved.

Watching a carefully filmed show about these places may make us want to visit these places someday, but it is a completely different experience than entering and interacting with them in person.

Day 286

Passively watching productions about wild places has value but can give us a false sense of understanding and mastery that will be quickly dispelled when we enter such a place in person. To lose a false sense of certainty and control in the face of a great reality is to be humbled.

This is what happens when we seek the presence of God, and when we face the prospect of unavoidable conflict with those God has placed in our lives.

If we let someone else engage the great realities for us to make the experience safer, more predictable and prettier, we essentially sever ourselves from us direct contact with our Creator and with the wisdom waiting for us on the other side of a struggle to deal with reality, which includes our differences.

Day 287

In wild places, we don't need to filter out nonsense because it is absent there. We are calmed by these places and with increased calmness comes increased clarity. When assessing how much we can learn in the time we have available; we start to sense it is inefficient to seek insight into God's solutions in cities.

Chances are, if we can't see the stars on a cloudless night, we are in a setting saturated with more contrived nonsense than divine wisdom.

Day 288

In each of these ecosystems, when we dedicate time and slow down, we can observe life solving problems in surprising and ingenious ways. By analogy we see types of challenges and the types of solutions nature uses to surmount each type of challenge.

These are the places humans do not dominate. They are not contrived theme parks designed to entertain us. Here there is real danger, and here we can easily make lethal errors.

Day 289

In wild places we must manage the possibility of real harm in an unfamiliar situation in which it is very likely we will make a mistake.

Here we are truly vulnerable and become intimately familiar with our primal human responses to feeling uncertain and unsafe.

Do we seek to run as far away as we can?

Do we seek to stay, but wipe out everything that could harm us, so we never need to feel vulnerable again?

Or do we realize this living system is also vulnerable? Do we feel admiration and respect and an instinctive desire to protect what we see?

In that sublime moment, in our chosen responses, we find the opportunity to begin humanity's story on earth all over again, but in a radically different way.

This time, we can stay aligned with and attuned to God's priorities as best we can understand them. We can remain open to having our understanding rearranged and upgraded with new information.

Day 290

In wild places we see that nature, for all its power and genius, is not designed to coddle us.

Historically, every attempt to eliminate all the small, local, ongoing vulnerabilities in a given location has ended up creating new, bigger, vulnerabilities.

For example, eliminating all small fires from a forest for 50 years will build up the fuel for a huge, much more destructive fire that is impossible to prevent.

Day 291

In wild places we are the students, not the teachers. Here we find inspiration, as we see it is possible for life to survive and thrive within non-negotiable limits that will not go away just because we want them to.

Rather than reject situational limits, in wild places we accept limits and learn to create something good within them – together. Productive togetherness itself is a function of accepting a set of ethical limits.

Day 292

If we look deeply into the examples God has already provided in the wild places across the earth, we will find patterns of interaction to inform our own new collective solutions.

If we slow down and take the time to watch, in wild places we find patterns of interaction to inform own new collective solutions,

Here we can learn how to stop seeing each other as the reason we can't reach our goals. We can stop standing nose to nose, opposing each other, and instead, turn and stand side by side and make the lack of a solution our common problem.

As we individually seek God in solitude, we can return to our relationship and start learning together what our situation has to teach us.

Here, in a wild place, all of us are quietly changed and instructed by an environment that is larger, older and wiser than any of us.

Day 293

In a forest we take in fresh air and feel refreshed. A natural byproduct of photosynthesis is oxygen, which all the other creatures of the forest require to survive. We benefit from what the trees no longer need.

Other creatures produce carbon dioxide as a natural byproduct of metabolism, which trees cannot survive without. Trees benefit from what their neighbors no longer need.

We start to sense that there must be ways we could help each other at little or no cost to ourselves. What one of us would have otherwise discarded without a thought could meet a critical need for someone with whom we share this space and time.

We are always on the lookout for these reciprocal benefit arrangements.

Day 294

God's genius is in all of creation. To encourage someone, we use words to acknowledge some part of God's genius that we see emerging in them. To honor another in this way is to honor our Creator who made them this way.

God placed in another person innate abilities you lack. When you acknowledge, name, and affirm the value of those abilities, you help them gain confidence that they belong here and serve a vital function. We affirm each other's unique value long before it is clear how all our abilities fit together to form a whole that serves God's purposes on earth.

We get more of whatever we acknowledge. Direct, face to face, verbal encouragement brings out more of each person's uniqueness. When we encourage each other we get to witness the unfolding of some attribute of God in someone's natural, unlearned, instinctive aptitude.

Day 295

In a relationship of mutual encouragement, we experience contact with God's genius more often. By using encouraging words, we cultivate the garden we ourselves live in. We help grow confidence in those around us who cultivate our own confidence in return.

In nature, the basic unit of life is not one individual life. Rather it is a community of individual lives that sustain each other. For example, we are able to digest our food only because we have a community of different kinds of microorganisms in our guts.

Communities of lives are sustained by emissions and absorptions, outputs, and intakes. Among humans, words are both emitted and absorbed, so we make the most of every word spoken, limiting them to the ones that are useful to God and helpful to our community of lives.

Day 296

Words are a form of social breathing. Our words can be as refreshing to each other as a walk in the forest. We think in words. When we observe a natural virtue in someone, the thought crosses our minds in the form of words.

We could just let the moment pass without saying anything, but by articulating what we see and value, using kind and gentle words, we freely emit something life-sustaining for another soul. It costs us nothing and means everything to them.

Our words are the most encouraging when they are emitted in person, face to face, in the immediate situation in which we observe something of God's goodness in another.

In this way we enrich our lives every day without spending any money.

Day 297

Being different from the majority and being undervalued for it, or being mistreated because of it, can cause us to feel a sense of shame.

The selfish majority may act like there is something wrong with us, or something wrong about us being here, which can make us doubt our own value. It is possible to internalize the rejection we feel from others and begin to reject ourselves.

God brings about a reversal in the experience of shame. The opposite of shame is not pride. The opposite of shame is a strength that comes from well-founded confidence.

We become convinced from our own first-hand experiences that God makes no mistakes.

Day 298

We become confident over time that what God placed in us at birth, and what God placed around us through the course of our lives, has been designed to activate and develop to its fullest what we were each created to be and do.

God is sovereign and does nothing without a purpose.

Just because we don't yet know God's purpose doesn't mean there isn't one or it isn't good.

The opposite of shame is not ego-inflating self or group affirmation. The opposite of shame is a deep and growing confidence in the reality and character of God, learned through real life experiences, not through doctrine or theory. It is a certainty that as we are restored to God's original design for humanity, we have a necessary and wonderful place in the unfolding story of life on earth.

Day 299

Mountain climbers encourage each other to get through the pain and fatigue and keep going. Mountain climbers help each other in situations where it is easier and safer to get to the next level up together than alone.

Within a culture of verbal encouragement and helpful cooperation, those who have felt rejected find respect, delight, and admiration for being different.

Here, among us, old wounds heal as we each develop the confidence to speak in our own voice. We start to freely contribute what God placed in us, and by doing so we enrich the life we share together.

Day 300

Diversity is about differences. Differences create tension. Tension often creates conflict.

Unresolved or poorly resolved conflict can stop the development of more diversity. Skillfully resolved conflict stimulates the development of more diversity. More diversity will at least temporarily create more conflict, which we deal with skillfully. This virtuous cycle is a delight to God because it opens the pathways of life to ever more life, which is ever more different.

We resolve conflict in a way that increases the stock of confidence and happiness among us, making us more adaptive and resilient than we were before the conflict appeared. As we do this we feel the warm delight and radiant presence of God among us in a way that no ritual or ceremony can match.

Day 301

Partnering with God to cultivate diversity means learning to resolve conflicts in a way that mirrors what we see in nature, which constantly creates networks of mutually beneficial, reciprocal relationships.

This network in turn allows more diversity to emerge, which again creates tension, and the cycle repeats. We are called to be peace-makers through collaboration, not through domination, avoidance, acquiescence, or by just reducing the amount of tension through messy compromises that satisfy no one.

Day 302

The gentle harmony, the functioning peace we see in a thriving natural system only arises through collaboration. Collaboration means putting as much effort into finding the best solution as we put into protecting and building our working relationships with each other.

We don't choose between getting it right and getting along. We do both with equal commitment and effort.

We build each other up. We don't tear each other down. It is not rational to weaken a teammate whose confidence and talent we ourselves will draw upon later.

We never stop getting better at solving problems by cooperating with each other. We never stop being a team and building the team.

Day 303

Where there is no teamwork, there will be no creative collaboration.

Where there is no creative collaboration there will be low or no diversity in ideas or actions – there will just be more of the same.

Where there is low or no diversity in ideas and actions there will be little creative tension or spontaneous movement.

Where there is little or no tension or movement there will be little or no innovation. If there are any surprises, they will rarely be good.

Where there is little or no innovation there will be no new pathways life can take to make its way through the big changes that have always been part of earth's story.

Where there are no new life pathways, there will be no new species.

Where there are no new species, there will be no new, unforeseen creative capacities God can use to continue the work of Creation.

Day 304

God continues to embed in creation the next installment of inexhaustible, unlimited divine intelligence.

Our part is to keep the gates of life open to the future so earth can become whatever God intends. We keep the gates of life open through repentance, ethical choices, growth and cooperation.

As faithful gatekeepers we get to see the genius of life itself pass through us and into the future.

Day 305

Each new unfolding of God's intention is more astonishing than the next because the form it takes is completely unforeseen, yet it makes total sense once we see it. Each divine solution is surprising, new, beautiful and useful, without waste.

Nothing human culture has ever imagined or created even begins to compare to the constantly unfolding creations of God. God does more.

In nature, more rarely means more of the same. In God's design, more normally means more divergence, more differences, more new forms, more new collective cooperative arrangements, more surprises, yielding ever more potential for more.

Essentially, when God does more God does more diversity.

Where there is increasing, thriving diversity, God is present and pleased.

Day 306

Everything good and new in nature starts out small, often growing very slowly for a long time, completely obscured by the bigger, older forms around it.

When something is small it is much easier to monitor its quality and make changes right where and when they are needed. God has not asked us to go big fast, but to create something that can last.

Our role models are not businesses or empires, but rather natural, long-lived ecosystems.

Day 307

Force and cunning will build something big quickly but will not create anything good that lasts because it is contrary to nature's laws.

Unrepentant, un-regenerating humans are insatiable for more but do more differently than God does.

Before repentance and regeneration humans do more by piling up more of the same, then working hard to hold onto it by eliminating diversity – which is a recipe for eventual collapse and extinction.

Day 308

The beginning of something new, different and better is a new, different and truer idea. The difference between old and new is another kind of diversity that requires another form of cooperation to manage productively.

Since our job is to optimize all kinds of diversity, we come to terms with the fact that there will always be both old and new ideas in the mix.

We manage this mix by seeking a better way to solve the problem at hand, one that is better than any humans have used in the past. The pattern for this new way is usually found in nature and helps us see what to take and what to leave behind in both our old and new human ideas.

Day 309

We don't honor the old so much that we leave no space for the new.

Neither do we honor the new so much that we leave no space for what has been learned in the past.

In nature, we see that life honors and protects the young above all else. But to do this, creatures make the most of whatever is available, including lessons learned from the past, to give their young the best chance at surviving and thriving in a changing environment - so that they will have a future.

Day 310

In nature, creatures learn new lessons in new situations and pass those on to their young.

Among us the older brother does not oppose the younger brother out of rivalry and envy but rather makes space for and protects his younger sibling who may someday bring new ways of adapting to the environment for his kind.

It is rational to protect the younger and newer, who bring fresh eyes to our changing situation, as they are more likely to find new pathways to a future for our kind.

Day 311

As a source of information to guide problem-solving and decision-making, inherited wisdom is more limited than the information that comes from first-hand experience. Receiving wisdom from the past typically involves no leaving home, no moving through new and perilous passages, no exploration and no experimentation.

First-hand experience is far more useful because it comes from decades of direct contact with the primary problems of existence and possible solutions for those problems.

Day 312

First-hand experience is hard-earned wisdom and carries with it natural authority. Maps are written by those who went to a new place first, then created something authoritative others can trust to go have their own new experiences in that new place more safely and productively.

Those that come after us can learn at our expense and start their own learning from there. Those with inherited wisdom only have not done primary work and have no right to be dismissive of new, earned wisdom. Rather, those with only inherited wisdom must sponsor those bringing new earned wisdom, form alliances with them and help complete and refine their work when needed.

Day 313

The difference between inherited and earned wisdom is first-hand struggle through the unsolved problems we all face in our current situation, as it is right here, right now.

Maintaining and preserving inherited wisdom requires a tiny fraction of the effort involved in gaining new, earned wisdom. Inherited wisdom only requires is hind-sight.

The best inherited wisdom can do is to perpetuate a solution that supposedly fit a situation that has long since passed, or theoretical situations that don't exist and have never existed. Inherited wisdom is a form of knowledge.

As valuable as it is, all knowledge is limited and most of it has an expiration date, when it is surpassed by new information.

Day 314

We distinguish between inherited and earned wisdom and give more standing to those who bring newly-earned wisdom.

Earned wisdom starts with imagination and insight into the patterns of nature, motivated by admiration of the Creator's genius and a desire to participate productively in creation.

Earned wisdom can be confirmed through proven, observable, results that can be replicated. Imagination is unlimited and the examples we find in nature are so vast and surprising they might as well be unlimited.

Earned wisdom comes from struggling through a current, real, changing, ambiguous situation without the benefit of hindsight, but rather with the benefit of ethical guidance from God, informed by the models available in nature.

Day 315

Our function as humans is to be the peacemakers who facilitate the growth of mutually beneficial arrangements between the different forms of life that constantly appear next to each other.

To be peacemakers we stay fluid in our responses. God's constant regenerating touch keeps us in a fluid state, able to move smoothly into the situations where differences cause friction, in the same way that oil reduces the friction between the moving parts of an engine.

Day 316

If the method someone advocates effectively limits selfishness and naturally cultivates helpful cooperation between us, even with all our differences, we know it comes from God and will be successful.

If the method someone advocates effectively rewards the most selfish person and makes us reluctant to gather to resolve our differences together, we know it is not from God and will not help us manage diversity.

A group of fluid cooperators can outcompete a group of rigid non-cooperators as long as the fluid cooperators can resist invasion by those who intend to receive help from others while providing no help in return.

Day 317

We refuse to allow defectors to become those among us who are admired as clever winners, taking without giving anything real in return.

We learn to spot the difference between a helpful giver and a selfish taker in the methods and means the person uses and advocates.

Just as our immune system recognizes and responds at once to a pathogen, not waiting until the disease is raging before attacking, we confront and stop unhelpful, selfish behavior the minute it shows up. Calculated selfishness will not gain a foothold among us.

Day 318

Groups are held together by emotional bonds. An emotional bond is essentially the desire to repeat an experience. We know an emotional bond has been broken when we have no desire to repeat a social experience.

We know there is a healthy emotional bond between two people when we see each imitating the other in some healthy, productive behavior and taking pains to coordinate their actions, so they don't cause preventable problems for each other. Imitation is the sincerest form of acceptance and admiration.

Day 319

When someone who is helpful and cooperative brings a new approach or method which solves a problem and produces better results, it is natural to want to repeat this experience and apply the method to other problems.

This is especially so if using the new method is more interesting than the way we used to do things. The new person and the new method are welcomed and happily included, their differences accepted and valued. We have formed a new bond with a new teammate.

We have experienced how God does inclusion in a community of lives.

Day 320

The more healthy and natural emotional bonds that form between individuals through the process of successful problem solving, the more cohesive and resilient the group becomes.

Embracing a wide range of useful adaptations is the essence of well-managed diversity that is essential for resilience.

Day 321

The more resilient a team is the more it can recover from a shock, from loss or setbacks, and the more it can adapt quickly to changing circumstances.

A more resilient team is a more confident team, willing to take on the next more challenging problem.

In this way what starts out as what seems like a dwindling minority of helpful, cooperative humans will one day be in the majority. This change in the composition of the species will happen because at some point nature selects cooperation as the way to survive, instead of selfishness. Cooperation is the only way a social species can overcome the challenge of a massive change in its environment.

There aren't many of us, there never have been. But we are the ones who will remain part of the story of earth.

Day 322

There comes a moment in problem-solving when no modification to our current understanding of God's way of doing things works.

Our approach no longer creates more justice out of diversity. It may only soothe the symptoms of an injustice, which temporarily masks the problem, but underneath resentment is festering.

Since we are intellectually and emotionally honest, we acknowledge we have made some kind of error. Sometimes it is just that what used to work no longer works because the situation has changed. Sometimes it is only a partial solution and now we need a more complete one, a shortcut that made sense then but left something out.

Day 323

There are willful errors and there are innocent, honest misunderstandings of the problem we are trying to solve. Willful errors come from believing we know better than God what is best and how things will turn out.

Innocent errors most often come from what is currently popular and unquestioned, even though it is unproven and typically contrary to how life solves problems in nature.

When we see that our solutions aren't working we stop and retrace our steps. We look for the point in our thought process where we added something dishonest or unjust or took a short cut that left out something true and necessary.

If the solution we have been using appears nowhere in nature it means God wouldn't have put it in, so we take it out. If the solution we have been using does appear in nature, it means God wouldn't have left it out, so we put it back in and start over, then see what happens.

If we don't make these corrections promptly, right when we sense the flow of life's fullness has slowed, we join those who will not remain on earth. By our negligence we prove ourselves unfit to remain.

Day 324

God uses diversity to ensure the future of a species by providing many optional ways to survive. Diversity is how God's rule spreads out in time.

Conversation is how God's rule spreads out in space, by providing many opportunities to catch and correct harmful errors before they are put into action. Conversation also leads to modifications and application of a good idea so that it can be applied to more situations.

The ultimate test of productive conversation is when we need to reason together to solve a problem and make a decision.

We demonstrate that God is regenerating our natural ability to cooperate with each other to the degree we can reason together in real-time through a difficult situation until we arrive at a solution that protects the needs of every member of our group.

The only reliable marker of divine regeneration is the ability to reason together under stress, when the problem we face impacts each of our interests, even though those interests are not the same.

Day 325

In nature, information is what causes something to happen that otherwise would not have happened. An example is the information encoded in our genes that directs cells to divide and create structures that would not have emerged otherwise.

As we are re-naturalized, we learn how to better preserve and transfer information that is still helpful to life or may be in the future.

The way to transfer basic information quickly to many individuals at once is called broadcasting.

Broadcasting behaviors exist in nature but are not used to create new pathways for life. In nature, a creature on occasion will broadcast a warning to all the creatures around it that a threat has appeared on the scene.

Receiving a broadcast message can be helpful in knowing how not to die in a time of crisis, but it is too general to help us know how to live the rest of the time. It is not the way nature transfers the intricate information used to create new patterns of life and new communities made up of diverse forms of life.

Day 326

Broadcasting information is limited because it is not the same as teaching and training. It can't make sure the information sticks and works well to address the many, varied and changing situations that define life on earth.

True understanding of an idea, and mastery in the application of it, comes through "narrow-casting."

Doctors, pilots, engineers and lawyers can't learn what they must learn about how to do the essential and stressful work they will do someday by watching or listening to broadcasts.

These are people who do work everyone else counts on. They build, operate and repair what all of us need to survive while living around each other. We lay our very lives in their hands and the lives of those we love.

When it really matters, we turn only to those who have mastered what they do in a different, harder, higher way, one that requires a lot more chosen effort invested over many years.

Day 327

The difference between the experience of receiving a broadcast signal and receiving a narrowcast signal is the prior experience of the recipient. A broadcast signal creates an experience for the receiver that requires little or no background. The more entertaining the signal the more it will be received.

A narrow cast signal creates a meaningful experience only for a recipient with deliberate prior learning already in place. The highly informed recipient will grasp the significance of a useful new idea and will know how to put it to use. The new idea may well be part of a breakthrough.

Breakthroughs reward long hours studying dense, difficult material followed by supervised practice and rigorous testing – for years. The rewarding feeling of a breakthrough is far greater, and lasts far longer than the enjoyment one can get from receiving entertaining, easy to grasp broadcast signals.

Day 328

Those who have invested sustained effort over years to understand something vital and complex are those who can make a new, significant contribution. This prior work requirement repels those who want things done for them, leaving only those rare few who genuinely desire to serve a purpose higher than their own personal gain.

Just as a magnet attracts if turned one way and repels if turned the other way, our founding work ethic gathers up small groups of those who are ready and willing to work together to do the task at hand, those who have no expectation that it will be easy or immediately gratifying.

In history, it is only small, devoted, working groups that have demonstrated the ability to prove to others that something new and different is doable and desirable. In this way small, local, self-organized groups come to re-define what is good and normal – the very basis of a new society.

Day 329

Two people, sharing the same situation, having mostly in person conversations is the main way information is transferred. It is the highest form of the narrow cast experience.

Broadcasting can be easily used to create uniformity and unanimity, a false and fragile form of unity. Conversational narrow-casting alone can eventually combine diversity into unity, which is the way the rule of God increases itself on earth.

Conversation and dialogue, in person, reasoning together through many difficult situations over many years - this alone can imprint God's way of doing things deep into the human heart until it is reflexive. This way of working together becomes more than what we do, it becomes who we are and who we are known to be by those outside our groups.

Day 330

We help to do happiness.

We move to do change.

We combine to do diversity.

We form the local safe spaces that can cultivate an endless unfolding of diversity, which is a delight to God. The safe space is a social structure, not a building.

The process of true dialogue improves all participating parties, making each more ready to face whatever situation they will face in the future. Even more importantly, this process makes the normal way we all treat each other better and more honorable, making our local group as a unit more fit to adapt to change quickly and effectively as needed.

Day 331

Saying something is true does not make it so. Writing something down and getting it published does not make it true.

The person who hears or reads an idea has questions, concerns, even objections, often very legitimate ones.

If the person speaking or writing is not there to see the recipient's response first-hand and cannot read the listener's body language and observe the listener's facial expressions, there is no way to clarify and correct any misunderstandings. The communicator also has no opportunity to discover errors in their own thinking or contradictions in their own behaviors.

This means there must be a corrective feedback loop in place that screens out error before it is put into action. Error enacted almost always ends up harming life in some way.

Day 332

In history messages sent out with uncorrected errors and messengers whose lives didn't embody their message have combined to create unnatural, unhealthy societies at war with other societies and with life on earth.

The way we avoid repeating that pattern of avoidable failure is to use ongoing, in person, two-way communication as our first and preferred way of gaining and using knowledge.

One-way communication can sometimes give someone an answer, but it is limited in its ability to demonstrate that we can find answers and solutions ourselves. Instead, it tends to cultivate passive dependence on an answer-giver and problem-solver.

Day 333

God' rule spreads slowly, through the quality of the experiences we have and the results we see. Those who create better experiences and get better results influence another, who goes on to influence another and so one. No form of mass media can do this because it is not real social and emotional contact.

Real contact is composed of reciprocal influence. If someone can get their ideas into your head, but there is no way to get your ideas into theirs, you are not in real contact, and the relationship is not a natural one.

We can only have a real, natural, reciprocal relationship with someone who is physically there for us in our time of need. These relationships are the natural pathway God uses to bring out new forms of life on earth.

Day 334

Occasionally in nature we see a wonderful mix of limited broadcasting and narrowcasting. There is a bat which lives in jungles that a flowering plant relies upon for pollination. The bat, flying at night, broadcasts a series of clicks out into the jungle, its signal hitting all the plants in front of it equally. But the plants don't all respond equally.

The particular flowering plant that relies upon the bat has evolved a large concave leaf that grows just below its' flower which is full of pollen. The leaf acts as a dish that collects and sends back a very concentrated echo of the bat's signal. The bat follows that strong echo right to the leaf, finds the flower, enjoys its rich nectar and gets covered in the flower's pollen. When the bat flies to the next plant of the same species, it pollenates that plant.

These books are meant to distribute our signal, but we know few will find them interesting or relevant. Only those whose previous life experiences have set them seeking something very different and better than what is currently available, will sense the value in these ideas. They will know how to respond and feel an urgency to do so.

Day 335

When it comes to the ideas in these books, it will be only those who have worked for years, struggling to offset the injustice and waste of the current civilization, who will respond.

Those who pick up on this signal will respond and move, not toward any gathering center or celebrity, but rather toward those living in their own immediate surroundings.

Stimulated by these ideas they will start fresh, new conversations with those they know and love.

As a social species, we are naturally capable of organizing ourselves and our efforts right where we are. We don't need or want a centralized organization to do that for us. We don't want or need a famous person to guide us. We are not in the business of following or creating celebrities.

God's new beginning will not come from the top down, from the outside in, with a big production. From our study of nature, we see that God does lasting, effective change very locally, from the bottom up, from the inside out, and from a beginning so tiny it is known only by those directly involved in it. The entire wonderful process of divine beginnings is closed to mere spectators.

Day 336

A tree needs sunlight. There is only one sun. So, a tree knows how to grow straight up to face the sun and does just that every day of its life.

A tree also needs water and nutrients. There are many and diverse sources of moisture and nutrients, in different concentrations and different places that constantly change, so a tree's roots know how to grow in, and every direction needed to obtain those resources.

Our conversations with God and each other follow the same design. We grow where we are placed, in one direction, toward God, and simultaneously many in directions toward the other lives around us. Our daily, primary conversation with God makes all the other conversations we have possible and functional.

Day 337

The tips of a tree's roots have a kind of brain that directs the growth of the root toward moisture and away from dryness, toward nutrients and away from toxins, toward soft soil and away from hard rock.

Roots find the resources the tree needs wherever and whenever they are available, making whatever adjustments are necessary to access them. Roots create reciprocal beneficial relationships with other forms of life such as fungi and bacteria. Each survives and grows because of what the other produces that it can't on its own.

The result is a circuitous network with roots twisting and turning in many surprising directions.

Day 338

We live our daily lives in a similar way to trees. Each day we seek the most direct, immediate contact with our Creator. Just as there is only one sun, there is only one Creator. We receive ethical instruction and direction to keep growing tall and straight.

Each day we also find and optimize the social and material resources available where we have been placed for now. We access these resources by creating mutually beneficial relationships with the other lives with whom we regularly share a space. We create and sustain these vital relationships through skilled conversation, built on careful listening.

We reason together, gathering facts, using logic, feelings and intuitions. We compare and combine different points of view. In this way our lives become deeply rooted, connected historically to life much older and larger than our own species.

Day 339

There are living conversations with a few people in our lives that last a lifetime. Conversations with others are shorter, but together they form the living fabric of our lives together as a social species.

Conversation performs the same function for a human society that a root system performs for plants. Real, deep, unrushed, unpackaged, spontaneous, ongoing conversations are the roots of a healthy relationship and become the root system to support the growth of a new civilization.

This societal root system cannot emerge from staged performances or ceremonies, from advertisements, or from recorded presentations or lectures. This is because the information exchange is only one-way; the communicator can get a message into the receiver's head, but the receiver cannot get a message into the communicator's head, so there is no error correction before action.

Day 340

Having truthful conversations is what builds the habitat for the diversity God loves.

Truthful conversations combine over many years to form a strong, stable and flexible base for the justice God expects.

God will sustain and protect human endeavors that create habitat and justice – and no other endeavors. There is no point in pouring our lives into something God won't support while it is being built or in defending it after it has been built.

Knowing this, we choose daily, no matter how frustrated or stressed we may be, to stay on God's side, and by God's side as we reason together to work our way through whatever difficulties we may face.

Day 341

Conversations that are...

intellectually and emotionally honest;

in-person so we can see each other's facial expressions and body language;

spontaneous, often prompted by the situation we share;

sustained over time;

rigorous, factual, logical, while staying empathetic and fluid...

These experiences alone have the capacity to build the royal highway along which The Sovereign Creator reenters and extends divine rule into the world, and out into the future.

(If the ideas in these books stimulate spirited conversations with others you trust and value, they serve their purpose. If these pages close conversations and become the final word, they are failing in their purpose. God alone has the final word on anything.)

Day 342

We have learned that when we go for quantity and the appearance of quick "success" we will get quantity and the appearance of success, typically very fast. But to do so we will have to skip the rich conversations needed to produce quality results.

In time, because of the poor quality of the lives gathered through sermons, speeches, lectures, mass media and staged performances, people sense the hollowness in it all and start to walk away or stay away in the first place.

By dismissing substance to get appearances, by ignoring quality to get quantity – in the long run we end up with neither quality nor quantity.

Day 343

Informed by the sober reality of past efforts to build societies based on quick quantity over slow quality, we 'choose to go for substance and quality, knowing we will not see results quickly. Love is patient. Greed is in a hurry.

We tell the truth. We do not say so much that there is no time left to hear anything new. We don't say so little that our conversation partner can't really use the information, because it is too vague.

We prioritize exchanging information that is relevant to the situation we both find ourselves in. We don't speak in riddles. Rather, we avoid being ambiguous and work to be as clear as possible. Avoidable confusion is too costly and risky to be given a place in the founding choices at the base of something new and better.

We accept high standards for conversation and dialogue, with those whom God put in our lives, as the only effective way to extend God's way of living in space and time. This is God's work, not ours.

We trust that this slow and careful way of building our society will produce enough of what God wants, just in time to set in motion whatever it is God has in mind next for life on earth.

Day 344

God works in vast time scales. If God's greatest concern is not how fast and far these governing ideas spread in our lifetime, it can't be our greatest concern either.

Since God is most concerned about how real and effective our individual and collective lives are, the quality of our interactions with each other is our greatest concern.

In nature complexity takes a long time to develop. Once complexity is in place it has the capacity to endure and grow for a long time because it is prepared to adjust to whatever challenges it meets.

Day 345

That which serves to strengthen the living, reciprocal exchanges between creatures also lengthens the life span of a living system. That which weakens living reciprocal exchanges also shortens its lifespan. The issue is not the raw strength of each individual creature, as every creature has strengths and weaknesses. The critical issue is the strength of the connections between all the creatures that share the same space and time.

Surprisingly, it is often the individually weakest creatures that do the most to strengthen these connections, and the individually strongest ones that do the most to damage them. What it takes to protect the apparently weak among us is exactly what it takes to protect the strength of our living network of interdependence.

Day 346

In nature, the more protective the environment, the more diversity we see. The harsher the environment, the less diversity we see.

In nature, the most fit creatures remain and flourish. Among social species the most fit are those that cooperate the best to protect all their members and even their neighbors.

The most fit creatures are the ones that make the most of diversity while wasting the least amount of resources.

A critical resource for the future is often hidden by God within the relationships we have not yet built with those whose abilities are different, and apparently less than our own.

Day 347

Differences in ability is another natural and necessary form of diversity. Each individual, no matter what abilities he or she has or lacks, is able to be useful to God and helpful to life.

We do whatever we can to help each among us see what was placed in them to serve God's purposes on earth and help them cultivate that gift to its fullest. We never give help that takes away dignity, just because we have an ability someone else lacks.

If we need the aid of others, we receive help graciously, without being touchy about it. Then we look for ways to be helpful in return, if only by making prompt and helpful observations about our shared situation. Sometimes those placed on the sidelines of action see things those in the middle of the action can't.

Day 348

It is God's intention that life on earth experience an unprecedented explosion of diversity. We were to be the species that alone can manage and optimize the astounding flourishing God has in store for all of creation.

In a regenerating state...

Working together as a society..

Under constant divine direction and correction...

Becoming ever more wise, ever more awake...

We are to become the catalysts of life on earth.

Day 349

A catalyst is something that increases the rate of interaction between other entities around without being used up, although it may be transformed itself.

A catalyst does not bring new forces to the mix to set off a chain reaction in a system. Rather, a catalyst unleashes and accelerates the forces that are already there. Some catalysts drop out after the unleashing and others stay in the mix.

We can't know ahead of time which one God has in mind for humanity. But either way we will have fulfilled the reason we exist and will know a joyful fulfillment that is inaccessible in any other way of living.

Day 350

God uses our interactions with others to release stored energy and direct it toward new, unforeseen productive ends. The energy we release is currently stored in the form of old certainties.

Early rockets used solid fuel. That was ok for fireworks but did not work for larger rockets that had serious work to do because it was impossible to precisely control the release of energy so that it could be increased or decreased in increments as needed.

Solid rocket fuel also packs too little energy per unit of weight, so a lot of it is needed to get the job done, which just adds more weight the rocket must lift and take with it on its journey.

Liquid rocket fuel worked better and made it possible to land on the moon. Liquid rocket fuel can be released precisely as needed and packs more energy per unit of weight. The rocket can use more of its energy going somewhere and less just fueling itself.

Day 351

Our old certainties work like solid rocket fuel, they are powerful, but unsuited to sustain precise, relevant adaptation to any and every situation we meet.

With old certainties we are either too certain of our response, regardless of the particulars in our situation, or we are not certain enough, because the tradition we cling to never imagined the kind of problem we face today.

With old certainties we either over respond badly, or we don't respond at all. Since in nature creatures that endure make neither of these mistakes, we can know something about clinging to old certainties is inconsistent with how God designed life to work.

With old certainties we also have to drag them around and make room for them everywhere we go, which only makes every task harder to do because they form one of the most common causes for pointless conflict between us and other, different lives.

Day 352

Using our lives as examples, God unleashes a different kind of energy that works like liquid rocket fuel. That fuel is made of personal and group insecurities.

We feel insecure when we fear losing something or not gaining something we are certain will make us happy and whole.

Unresolved insecurity creates a sense of shame in an individual or group. We feel there might be something wrong with us if we can't ever feel secure in a way that it seems others do. Feeling somehow defective is deeply threatening to our sense of self, to our dignity.

Day 353

God never intended any individual or group to feel defective and ashamed. In order to finally transform any insecurity into dignified confidence, God must first bring it to light, where it can be touched and healed.

We take turns confronting the errors we see in each other's thinking and methods.

As long as we do so ethically and honorably, both sides feel safe enough to reveal outlived certainties and insecurities.

This releases bottled up energy that we can use to build a new society between us that makes the most of the differences God put in us.

Day 354

The transformation of old certainties into a new vital connection to God, nature, and each other only happens when we find ourselves in real situations when there is a lot at stake.

This transformation cannot happen by engaging in abstract, theoretical, discussions about hypothetical situations, because all parties to a conflict know it is not real and there is no real possibility of loss, so they will not be fully invested emotionally in the work.

Only under stress do our insecurities come out. Under stress we regress – often to some version of how our parents coped with stress, or to the way we did as kids.

Day 355

Only when we are engaged in a real, vital situation, with our interests at stake are we fluid enough to change. Stress creates openings, cracks in our certainties. We can go through those cracks and finally become someone who stops resisting whatever God is doing and starts helping whatever God is doing. We learn to behave this way even though we can't be certain ahead of time what it is God is up to.

Using the stress of real situations in which we must make decisions, God surfaces and then re-solves deep, legitimate fears. Until now our old certainties had masked and soothed these fears, but never really resolved the issues causing them.

Stress loosens the masks and let's God touch our lives in ways we never could have imagined. The result is a deep, grateful love. We emerge with a deep trust we take into our next insecurity-inducing situation, which will surely appear. Though this repeated cycle strength is added to strength. Confidence is added to confidence, in ourselves, in each other, and in our team.

We experience ourselves becoming a creative force of nature.

Day 356

We treat other lives the way God has treated us. God is our highest model, whom we imitate. We solve the problems of our shared existence the way other, long-lived species do. We imitate nature's solutions.

Imitation is limitation. To do what someone else is doing means not doing something else I could have done instead. When imitating a model that is more complex and capable than us, we stop doing some things we used to do. Only later do we realize how harmful those behaviors were. When imitating, we trust as a way of knowing instead of knowing everything first, before we trust.

Imitation is the surest evidence of a bond between two lives and is the highest form of approval.

What we learn to stop doing is even more important than what we learn to start doing. If we leave uncooperative, destructive, selfish behaviors in place, they will cancel and destroy any new creation we may attempt.

Day 357

When we adopt a model, we take seriously the real limits in our situation and limits to our responses to our situations. Wanting to be like our model, we restrain impulses to do something we used to do. Most often, any impulse we are limiting is powerful, natural and necessary.

Limiting is not eliminating. It is not condemning and rejecting. It is not harmful to have the impulse, passion or drive, but by mismanaging it we would end up harming ourselves and others.

Day 358

By restraining a strong natural impulse its power does not go away. Rather, its power is transferred back to us, both individually and as a working group. This returning force acts to pull us together into a higher form of complexity. We become stronger and more resilient, more ready to respond – like a coiled spring. Our minds become more integrated, rather than being divided and neutralized by opposing drives.

Within the limits set by our model, our relationships become more cooperative. We are no longer beset by exhausting and pointless quarrelling.

Day 359

"More" is about increase.

In nature increase comes through more difference; more diversity. To want more is to want more diversity. Once we function as ethical catalysts, we will see the unfolding of more diversity and complexity at an ever-faster rate.

More diversity and complexity will create more tension and friction, initially. And just bigger engines use more oil than smaller ones to reduce the friction and heat, there will be more need for our kind as God's intentions unfold and flourish. Our job is to bring peace out of the differences.

Peace is the name of the happiness that catches up to us when we are making sure each of God's creatures has what they need to become all God intended them to be.

We embody the justice of God in our lives. Justice becomes normal behavior among us. Peace is the fruit, the natural product of justice.

Day 360

The evolution of life is a result of new combinations.

Every creature has a God-given right to evolve by learning how to combine what it does with new and different ways of doing things. Our role, when life needs help finding its way, is to make sure there is no artificial limit to the options available to life, when life needs help finding its way.

When another life calls out for help, it is signaling that it needs to combine with something it cannot produce itself. If help is not forthcoming, there will be no new combination. If there is no new combination, there is no evolution.

We are here to help all of God's creatures find what they need next to meet the challenges of a changing planet. We are here to help creatures combine their differences in ways that help themselves, other creatures, and the larger environment they share.

Day 361

I am not like the moon in most respects, yet the invisible forces that hold me in my seat as I write these words, are the same ones that hold the moon in its orbit around the earth.

The way we help new combinations emerge is to see, with patient eyes, the few essential common needs which otherwise different lives share. What they share in common for a least a period of time in their lives, is what makes them alike, while everything else about them makes them different the rest of the time. Common needs are often episodic, not constant. That is why we need a patient eye to see over the course of a life what others will need eventually.

Meeting these few episodic needs when they are acute is essential to the continuing evolution of life. Pursuing non-essential needs divides us and pits us against each other. Working to meet essential episodic needs unifies us and turns us into allies, by creating a healthy interdependence, a standing readiness to be there for each other when our moment of need arrives.

Day 362

An example of an essential episodic common need is the need for rest and refueling. All living things have times of energy expenditure and times of energy replacement. Without a place of repair and refueling, all lives end, and all living systems collapse.

With a safe and peaceful place of repair and refueling, most lives and most living systems can recover and adapt to whatever comes next.

Day 363

Another example of an essential episodic need common to otherwise very different lives is the need for protection during life transitions.

All living things are very vulnerable when they pass from one stage of life to the next. This is when living things need help the most. We help each other manage that vulnerability.

By providing protection and sustenance during life transitions for the creatures we know personally, we do more to cultivate diversity than almost anything else we can do.

Day 364

Our job is not really that hard or complicated. God does not set us up to fail.

Ours is a work of elegant simplicity.

We take the time to sense and then protect the few essential things diverse lives require. From there, life can take care of itself. We don't so much protect individual lives or types of lives, as we protect the reciprocal connections between different lives, so they can protect their own lives and their own way of life.

When connections that support episodic interdependence are healthy, everything life can do happens over time. While living alongside a thriving but different type of life, new and better options become available. Neighbors can adopt the most useful and attractive methods they see from others around them.

We form new combinations peacefully, freely, by choice, not by force. Like all other living things, we naturally add to our lives what promises more life and lives up to its promise.

Day 365

When we are doing our work of peace, what can still emerge does emerge.

The saddest thought is what could have been but never got the chance to exist. God grieves over that which could have happened on earth which human society prevented. By creating societies organized around unlimited selfishness, humans stopped the emergence of other possible ways of life.

We defend the right of all lives to combine with whatever and whoever helps them evolve into whatever they need to be next. We defend the right of all lives to realize their God-given creative potential.

God delights in all that can unfold, all that can become real that hasn't yet emerged. God never stops creating and we help the process by insuring justice for all of life, with all its differences.

It is then that we live in the warm glow of God's delight.

Epilogue

"It is the duty of all people to seek after truth and to uphold it in the face of opposition."

- Welsh Proverb

Spend time roaming in an environment where nature is doing what it does the way it does it and has been doing it for a long time. You will come across very old paths. These have been created by animals making their way from one place they need to be to the next place they need to be. The land the path crosses is probably owned by someone or some entity. That does nothing to stop animals from using the old paths or creating new ones if they need to.

How did animals make their paths? They just did it. By exerting themselves, using their own energy. Without formal permission. Without anyone noticing. In history, these ancient animal paths have become human paths, then roads, then highways.

There is a piece of real estate that is more valuable than all the property on earth combined. It is the human mind's conception of what is true, dependable and good. Large, powerful, old human institutions claim to own this mental real estate – the space called "values." Look what they have done with it! Do you see truthful, good behavior that will surely lead to a higher state of well-being for all life on earth? No - their "values" have never created what we see in nature – the combination of both high diversity and high organization, the only arrangement that is peaceful, evolving and sustainable.

For this reason, we don't wait for approval and permission from any human authority to start over and do something new, different and better, to do diversity God's way. We just do it. We think for ourselves and choose our own actions. We enter the niche God has created for us and make our way, demonstrating a better way exists to both survive and thrive that does not harm others or their habitat. We put a lot of time and effort into it. We see possible and promising new combinations, then help them happen.

By taking the approach migrating animals use, we demonstrate that we value this mental space more than those who currently claim the right to control it, those who tell us what to think and do. By producing quiet, consistently growing, good results we earn the right to stay. This mental space we carve out and share between us comes to define who we are and explain why we're here.

We are the peace makers.

Those of us who are different, who see things differently, who have different ultimate values and aims, are agents of the True Owner of earth, including the space called "values." As agents, we have all the permission we need. We take up our delegated task and add patience to divinely guided effort. We won't inhabit much physical space on earth in our lifetimes. We are a small and highly dispersed people, but we are the kind of humans that will inherit and inhabit earth's future.

Earth's future is open to us because we are open to God. We are called to make the years that lie ahead new, different and much better than anything that has gone before. The plans will come from God, unfolding daily in the form of the small adjustments only a loving person is willing to make. The surprise and delight in discovery will be ours. The glory will go to God alone, because the work will turn on unforeseen openings only God can create, aided by the full force of nature.

Let the work begin.

Cordially,

Tim Daniel

www.ingramcontent.com/pod-product-compliance
Lightning Source LLC
Chambersburg PA
CBHW070609030426
42337CB00020B/3722